In Search of
MAN
ALIVE

Roy Bonisteel

In Search of
MAN
ALIVE

COLLINS, Toronto 1980

First published 1980 by
Collins Publishers
100 Lesmill Road, Don Mills, Ontario

Canadian Cataloguing in Publication Data

Bonisteel, Roy.
  In search of man alive

ISBN 0-00-216815-4

1. Biography - 20th century. I. Man alive (Television
program) II. Title.

CT120.B66   920'.009'04   C80-094713-4

Printed in Canada.

To
   Mandy,
      Steven
         and
            Lesley
with love and respect

*The glory of God
is in man
fully alive.*

St. Iraneus.
2nd. Century

ACKNOWLEDGEMENTS

I would like to thank the Current Affairs Department of the Canadian Broadcasting Corporation for permission to quote from transcripts of several *Man Alive* programmes, also for the use of their research library to check facts and data.

Thanks also to Michael Worek for his encouragement and assistance in preparing this book.

Special thanks and appreciation to my wife Jane for her editorial assistance in preparing the manuscript and for her constant love and unfailing support at all times.

CONTENTS

In Search of
MAN
ALIVE

PREFACE

Increasingly, during my years with *Man Alive*, people across the country have asked, "Why don't you write a book? You've been so many places, interviewed so many interesting people. We would enjoy reading about it very much."

For a long time I thought it was just people I met saying kind things. I have found viewers go out of their way to be generous in their comments and magnanimous in their criticisms. Those of us who work in television are much more critical than the viewers, who always seem to be hoping for the best and really expecting us to do better next time.

It wasn't until several publishing companies began to ask me to write a book about *Man Alive* that I decided to try. After all, thirteen years is a long time for any prime time weekly programme to survive, but it is unheard of for it to last that long when the subject is religion. No other religious programme in the world has managed to exist for nearly as long in a prime time slot. The number of people watching any programme is always of great concern to the networks. In order to do the least damage possible to the ratings, most religious programmes are buried in the Sunday morning "ghetto," that's six a.m. to noon. Usually, only a religious "special," such as a Billy Graham crusade, can attract enough viewers to be shown during the evening hours.

The only religious television programme, prior to *Man Alive*, ever to successfully hold down a prime time spot was *Life Is Worth Living*, the late Bishop Fulton Sheen's programme which was popular in the 1950's. Bishop Sheen was articulate, intelligent and witty. He did not talk down to his audience or scream at them. When his audience wavered and diminished, Sheen lost his sponsor and was taken off the air. No matter how high the quality of a show, American networks are not in the business of subsidization. Their programmes must attract sponsors, which in turn create profits for the networks.

The Canadian Broadcasting Corporation, however, supports non-sponsored programmes. That's why a series such as *Man Alive* or *Marketplace* can remain on the air. They are valuable in terms of content even though they may not command millions of viewers. There is no opportunity for them to generate revenue because CBC policy does not allow news or current affairs programmes to be sponsored, a regulation with which I am in total agreement.

Once ratings or commercial considerations become the main concern of a programme it loses its integrity, often becoming more cautious, certainly less reliable. While the American networks have come a long way from the days when Tennessee Ernie Ford was not allowed to appear on the Dinah Shore show because she was sponsored by Chevrolet, the real danger of client pressure is still there.

Some American and Canadian religious programmes are "sponsored" in one sense. The client is the evangelists' own organization. His crusades are advertised, so are his universities, his records and books. These multi-million dollar businesses prosper and expand under the umbrella of religion.

Sig Gerber, Executive Producer for the CBC Current Affairs Department and former *Man Alive* producer used to say jokingly, "Roy, let's quit working so hard on topics that are complex and difficult to communicate. With your image and my production ability we could clean up in the evangelical television market." No doubt we could have, but neither of us would have been able to live with our consciences. The worst part, of course, would be the enslavement to only one point of view and the terrible burden of always having "the answer."

The joy of doing *Man Alive* is in the diversity of views presented on a wide range of subjects. While some people we interview may claim to have the solution to a particular problem, the viewer is always given a chance to apply his own experience and intelligence to the question at hand. One loyal *Man Alive* viewer wrote, "what I like about your show are the surprises. I never know what to expect. It differs so, from one week to the next."

In any given season *Man Alive* viewers can weigh and evaluate the words of a soft spoken, almost ethereal Jean Vanier with the crisp, no-nonsense scientific mind of Viktor Frankl or Barbara Ward. They can trace the history and discover the mystery of their own faith through dialogue with theologians of every creed. On the theory that no one has all the answers and no sect or denomination is perfect, *Man Alive* strives to dig deeply into the many expressions of spiritual thought, hopefully casting light on moral and ethical truths.

The *Man Alive* cameras have found me interviewing representatives of a wide spectrum of religious thought, from Archbishop Anthony Bloom and Mother Teresa, to the Western Guard and the Irish Republican Army. The theologically conservative Rex Humbard and Billy Graham have shared air time with Archbishop Ted Scott and Hans Küng. Religious activists like the Berrigan brothers, Helder Camera, Father Groppi and Dorothy Day have taken their turn with Pat Robertson, Cardinal Spellman, Dr. Edward Norman and Anita Bryant. The list seems endless. The subjects stretch out over thirteen years of half-hour, one night stands. Which ones should be called back to take another bow through the pages of a book?

Almost every viewer I meet has a favourite *Man Alive* programme. Many viewers were moved by the programmes I did in Africa in 1975 and the one in Belfast in 1974. None of these are included here. The strengths of these programmes were timeliness and visual quality, strengths that cannot be captured in this book.

In these pages I have written about several of the older programmes which may, at first glance, seem dated and passé. They do, however, reflect an important era in society and our religious attitudes at that time. A glance back shows our programme titles kept pace and often led the news stories of the day. After all, according to the headlines and magazine covers, God lived, died and was born again during the *Man Alive* years.

And what has all this done to me? That's the question I am asked by every interviewer. It was also posed by publishers who expected a chapter titled, "I found my faith in Studio Four." The fact of the matter is that any change in me or my beliefs must be reported by my colleagues, or my children, or someone who has known me during these years. As far as I know I'm still a broadcaster, a reporter, a curious mind wondering about a possibility; a searcher, exploring other people's findings, a conduit bringing thoughtful messages into the lives of Canadians who care enough to change the channel to "something entirely different."

I love television, but I love its potential not its performance. It is basically a young medium, but it already suffers from a senescence of gigantic proportions. It has aged prematurely. It has become bland and trite for the most part. Now and again it hits the mark, with a programme that provides food for the famished mind, insight into a hopeless situation, hope for an abandoned ideal. At that moment this strange invention becomes more than a box full of tubes and wires, a message more than a medium, the reason I continue in the search for worthwhile programmes that give pride to my profession and satisfaction to my standards. Some of these moments we have captured on *Man Alive* and I would like to share them with you in this book.

My selection has been highly subjective. These are the programmes I enjoyed for more than one reason. Some were milestones in religious programming, some were influential in changing people and society, some were just a lot of fun to do and gave great pleasure to my viewers.

FOREWORD

I am often asked questions such as, "How did you think of this programme idea?" or "How long did it take you to edit this show?" These questions are asked by people who are not familiar with television production and therefore attribute each step to me.

If you were to dissect any given *Man Alive* programme you would uncover as many people involved as would be found in an average sized company. These people carry out jobs not always equated with the television industry.

The invaluable office staff answer the telephones, handle the correspondence, type the scripts, and keep track of what everyone else is doing. *Man Alive* has been extremely fortunate to have had the same secretary, Bertha McMullen, for many years. She has helped provide a sense of continuity to the department.

Then there are the production assistants. They function as knots which tie the many elements together. They reserve studio and production facilities, order the necessary art work, attempt to keep the shows running on schedule and fill in wherever the producer needs "assistance." They are the direct link between the performer and the producer during the whole process. It has been said that this is the most difficult job in the industry, ably handled currently by Eric Lipka and Mary Munson.

Researchers provide information about the guests, expand story ideas and provide new ideas by reading more publications than I would have thought possible.

The Unit Managers represent the administration within a production "unit". It is their job to approve budgets, work out the details of all money matters and deal with the upper management in virtually all areas, excluding programme content. Gail Cochran, *Man Alive's* Unit Manager, has saved the day on more than one occasion by supplying much needed emergency funds.

Before any programme is aired, each person has to perform his job properly or the results would be immediately obvious to the viewer. This includes the graphic artists, set designers and decorators, make-up artists, lighting technicians, cameramen, soundmen, switchers, video control, cue prompter operators, sound effects people, telecine, video tape operators and editors, technical producers, film editors, re-recording technicians and ALL their assistants. I sincerely hope I haven't left any area out, but as you can see there are a vast number of people involved.

I have left to last the people ultimately responsible for the programme as a whole: the producers.

In the early years of *Man Alive* the production load was carried by a very small staff of producers, primarily, Maggie Watchman, Dave Ruskin and John Ryan. The style then was to incorporate three or four different segments, produced separately, into each half-hour.

As we adopted a single theme for each programme the production staff grew. Over the years it included such talented individuals as: Garth Goddard, Terri Thompson, Sig Gerber, Sam Levene, John McGreevy, Louise Lore, Tim Bentley, Rosalind Farber, Katherine Smalley, Myles White, Wayne Thompson, Tom Kelly, Azza El Sisi and Don Cummings.

Many producers brought their own special interests to the programme. Just two examples were John McGreevy, who gave us his brilliant dramatic portrayals of historic figures who changed the course of religious thought, and Sig Gerber, whose compassionate and insightful documentaries on Canada's native people reflected his own caring and concern.

There were also several CBC producers from other departments and freelance producers from outside the Corporation who contributed many outstanding programmes.

Overseeing all of this were two men who guided us through thirteen years of weekly programming. The Reverend Brian Freeland, religious advisor to the CBC, and Leo Rampen, executive producer. Leo's job was recently assumed by Louise Lore as he moved to become director of English Language Television for the CBC in Quebec. On his shoulders fell the final responsibility for the series. His encouragement and professional ability helped producers develop and bring to fruition many a complex project. He became, for me, a constant source of support and,more important, a valued friend.

Brian Freeland is the rudder that keeps us all on course. His theological insights and quiet insistence on excellence have been basic to the success of *Man Alive*.

So, when a viewer writes to say thanks for "my" show the credit really must go to all these people behind the scenes.

FROM THE GHETTO
TO PRIME TIME

*My approach to the church was, "Tell me
what you want to say, and I'll show
you how to say it."*

On one of Stan Freberg's last radio shows in the 1960's he tried
to explain to a ten year old girl what radio was like in the "good
old days" of the 1940's.

"We had actors, and sound effects, and orchestras," he says.
"We had programmes of drama and comedy."

"But what did you look at?" asks the child.

"You didn't look at anything," answers Freeberg. "You used
your imagination."

"Boy," exclaims the girl, "talk about your radical ideas."

While many still remember the old radio shows, a great number of Canadians have grown up knowing only the "music and
news" format of the modern medium. I was part of the industry
during it's transition.

I began my radio career in Belleville, Ontario in 1951. The
station in which I worked still carried a few of the big American
network programmes. Edgar Bergen and Charlie McCarthy, Jack
Benny and Bing Crosby, were available direct from the American

networks, as were some of the old afternoon soap operas. Television's impact on radio drama and comedy, however, was swift. By 1953, when I moved to CKTB, St. Catharines, Ontario, the private networks had practically abandoned all attempts to produce the kind of "imagination programming" that had been radio's mainstay for twenty-five years.

Radio frantically revamped formats in a desperate attempt to halt the complete transformation of "listeners" into "viewers." Surveys purported to prove that a radio listener's attention span had been reduced to two minutes. Programmes became shorter. The pace quickened. Newscasts became summaries, then bulletins. Discussions and interviews gave way to the three "t's," time, temperature and traffic reports. The disc jockey was king and the faster his spiel the better. Dead air was a sin. Soon, all that remained of old style radio were the religious programmes. The transcribed dramas from the Lutherans, the Salvation Army and the "Christophers" became listener stumbling blocks. The slow paced devotional and meditation programmes sent listeners dial-twisting and the hour-long church service became an embarrassment to ratings conscious stations.

Canadian broadcasting regulations required that religious broadcasting be included in the station's schedules. Clearly, something had to be done for the sake of both the industry and the church.

Over the years the most frequent question I'm asked is "Why did you first get into religious broadcasting?" Frankly, the reason was to improve the quality of the programmes in order to command decent ratings. The church had to look at itself as a commercial client, with religion as its product. I met with clerical groups of various persuasions explaining that their concerns should parallel the radio station's; that is, reaching the largest number of people in the most effective manner. "Not only does your format need changing," I told them, "but the time has come to stop dividing the audience with denominational programming. Since you are all basically saying the same thing, select the better broadcasters among you and let them do the on-air work, on an inter-denominational basis."

How naive I was. I was aware of professional jealousy in broadcasting, but that was nothing in comparison to the competition between "men of the cloth." The radio ministry of many individual clergymen, though not very effective in terms of "spreading the gospel," was an ego trip that few would relinquish. Their broadcasts remained unchanged.

I had more success with broadcast workshops, training ministers to tone down their gothic-like pulpit voices for sensitive studio microphones, and to write crisper, less pompous material. Some became very adept at preparing one-minute "thoughts for the day," once they got over their surprise that it didn't take a thirty minute sermon to say "God is love."

I was with CKTB until 1964 when I left to present an application to the Board of Broadcast Governors for a new radio station license in St. Catharines. During the lengthy hearing I produced radio programmes and commercials, managed public relations campaigns and did a variety of freelance broadcasting work.

The Reverend Keith Woollard, head of broadcasting for the United Church of Canada, heard of my attempts to improve the quality of religious radio and asked if I would become an advisor to the church in this area. Berkeley Studio, the United Church's production centre, has a long and distinguished reputation in film, radio, and television production. The secular broadcasting industry recognizes the technical quality of its programmes and the experimental nature of its material. At this time, Woollard and his department of broadcasting, were still reeling from the public reaction to their introduction into Canada of the first commercial jingle advertising God. Produced by the multi-talented Stan Freberg in Hollywood, these one minute spots used dramatic situations to pose modern dilemmas, then ended with a swinging chorus asking what it's like to be "out on a limb — without HIM." Freberg signed off the tag himself with a punchy "the preceding was brought to you by the United Church of Canada." Many church members considered this too crass and some radio stations refused to run the commercials. To me it meant that at least one denomination understood how to use radio effectively.

Working with the Berkeley Studio staff, I produced the quarter-hour program *Checkpoint*, a crisp blend of interviews and modern music, touching on contemporary social issues. This programme was picked up, on a regular basis, by ninety-four private stations. The industry was quick to welcome religious programming that would help fulfill its obligation to the Bureau of Broadcast Governors, later the Canadian Radio-Television and Telecommunication Commission, while at the same time holding an audience and improving ratings.

Requests for broadcast training and production workshops were coming in to Berkeley at an increasing rate from ministers across the country who wanted to make better use of the air time provided by local stations.

At last the two concerns were aligned. The aims of both the station and the church were being met.

One of the most interesting challenges was CKWX in Vancouver. This station was originally owned by the United Church. It had subsequently been sold to secular interests, but the church had retained four hours a week for religious use. The British Columbia broadcasting committee of the United Church asked if I would be interested in producing the programmes necessary to fill this time, and also expand the church's exposure on both radio and television throughout the rest of the province.

With Woollard's encouragement, I accepted the position of Director of Broadcasting for the United Church in British Columbia and for the first time became involved in religious television production as well as radio.

The scope of the work in British Columbia and the challenges it presented convinced me to give up the radio station application in St. Catharines. Many of my broadcasting colleagues were surprised and somewhat amused that I had become involved full time in religious broadcasting. After all, I had no theological training. I was not a regular church goer, and except for some earlier work with a youth group in St. Catharines, had very little contact with the field of religion. In many ways this was an advantage. The industry knew and trusted my programming judgment. There was never a lack of air time for quality productions. My approach to the church was, "Tell me what you want to say, and I'll show you how to say it." The major problem was that at this time, in the mid-sixties, the church had great difficulty deciding what it wanted to say. Ferment was everywhere. I have often reflected that, with the possible exception of the Reformation, I couldn't have picked a more exciting and challenging time to become involved with religion. Indeed, the church was going through a new reformation. Pope John XXIII's "opening of the church windows" during Vatican II had sent a draft through the entire structure. Priests and nuns became more accessible to the media. The Pope himself said that if St. Paul were alive today he would probably be a journalist. Newspaper religion editors found their stories turning up on the front page instead of between the church ads and the obituaries. Radio talkshow hosts found themselves juggling callers' questions concerning faith with criticisms of the sewer system. But it was books by critics of the church establishment that made the greatest impact.

Bishop of Woolwich, John Robinson's *Honest to God* became a best seller in and out of church circles. It was written in 1963, but responses to it, in the form of other books, reviews, articles and debates continued the dialogue for years. It was compared with the nailing of Luther's thesis to the church door at Wittenburg and its revelation of the secret erosion of the supposed canons of Christian belief shocked or delighted readers depending on their theological stance. In the United States the following year *Time* magazine devoted a major part of one issue to describing the Christian renewal already underway, the church's openness to radical change and its alliance with secular society. Bishop James Pike, already in trouble with the Episcopal hierarchy, wrote *A Time For Christian Candor* outlining a faith bogged down with non-essential dogma, morés, customs and traditions. Then in 1965 came *The Comfortable Pew* by Pierre Berton, a unique publishing experiment commissioned by the General Board of Religious Education of the Anglican Church of Canada. Not only was an outsider writing a scathing critique of the church, but the church itself was asking him to do it. In his foreword to *The Comfortable Pew* Reverend Ernest Harrison, who approached Berton to undertake the project, said, "There has been much talk about the need for the church to listen. We have shown a grand talent for lecturing and hectoring; but we seem unwilling to believe that God works through men outside our ranks, who may have much to teach us and a few legitimate challenges to make."

The Comfortable Pew broke all existing Canadian publishing records and was praised and damned from pulpits across the country.

These books, along with *The Secular City* by Harvey Cox, *God's Frozen People* by Mark Gibbs and *A Church Without God* by Ernest Harrison were my introduction to the world of religion, my theology primers. It was pretty heady stuff and I never lacked for fresh and relevant radio or television material. Religious broadcasting was dull no longer.

It seemed, strangely enough, that the church was beginning to enjoy the abuse. At seminars, teach-ins, and even regular diocesan and presbytry meetings, the strongest critics of the church received the loudest ovation. The United Church Board of Evangelism and Social Services for example, flew in Saul Alinsky, militant social reformer from Chicago, to accuse the clergy of "hate, bitterness and diabolical unkindness." Eric Nicol, June Callwood, Arnold Edinborough, Pierre Berton and others were commissioned by the United Church to write a book of criticism entitled *Why The Sea Is Boiling Hot*. Among other things they branded the church as money hungry and uncaring. Important Roman Catholics, Anglicans and members of other traditional churches seemed eager to get into print and on the air to debate "our church is worse than yours."

Individual congregations smiled and nodded as their clergy berated them for being in church instead of on the picket line. Amplifiers and tape machines replaced the minister in front of the church altar. Members listened and discussed Bob Dylan's "With God on Your Side" or "It's All Right Ma" which accused them of worshipping "flesh coloured Christs that glow in the dark."

There was a frantic rush to be relevant by clergy of all denominations and the media became their best ally. Every day my mail was full of invitations to cover the latest clergy supported love-in, protest rally, freedom march or experimental service. Religion was news. Because of my "foot-in-both-worlds" position I was constantly being tapped by the media to find them a "militant priest," a minister who marched at Selma, or a nun who was leaving her order in protest.

Generally, I refused because this kind of sensational reporting of surface discomfort didn't do justice to the deep rebirth pangs the church was going through. I did, however, accept assignments from both CBC and CTV to conduct more in-depth interviews with contemporary theologians who were addressing the larger issues. These included, Dr. Robert McAfee Brown, the perennial Protestant observer of the Roman Catholic scene and Bishop James Pike, whose California heresy trial was attracting world-wide attention.

The social issues of the day were bringing denominations and faiths together in common actions. In this new found spirit of ecumenism, I was able to try out my ideas for shared broadcasts. After a series of discussions with Father Ed Bader, Director of the Catholic Information Centre in Vancouver, Reverend Art Hives, Regional Director of Communication for the Anglican Church and Reverend Jack Shaver, United Church Chaplain at the University of British Columbia, I cancelled the weekly church service from CKWX and launched a freewheeling open-line programme called *God Talk* in its place. The public responded enthusiastically. The programme became a sounding-board for religious expression that continued for many years after my departure.

This experimental kind of programming did not stop there. With the help of two young Vancouver broadcasters, Brian

Brenn and Jim Morrison, a weekly magazine programme called *Dateline* was produced for twenty radio stations throughout the province. Father Bader and I had seen the need for this on a visit to the stations in the spring of 1966. The idea was to provide a current affairs show with a spiritual dimension, tackling the issues of the day from a moral and ethical standpoint. Stations scheduled *Dateline* in mid-week prime-time slots. At last religious programming had broken out of the Sunday morning ghetto. Another first developed when, as my costs began to exceed my budget, stations offered to help pay for the production costs.

As far as possible I kept all my work ecumenical, whether it was programming, broadcast training or media-clergy workshops. Despite the fact the United Church footed the bill for the entire operation, I operated under the umbrella of Inter-Church Broadcasting, encouraging the co-operation and involvement of many other denominations. Remi de Roo, Roman Catholic bishop of Victoria and Ted Scott, then bishop of the Kootenays, later Primate of the Anglican Church of Canada, were enthusiastic and helpful supporters of Inter-Church broadcasting.

Television also continued to be a concern of the traditional churches. Reverend Des McCalmot of the United Church, Reverend Peter Meggs of the Anglican Church and Father Frank Stone of the Roman Catholic Church were already working as a team on television projects for both networks and private stations. The national communication offices of these three communions decided, in 1967, to appoint a co-ordinator for their radio operations and offered me the position. This meant I would be working officially for all three churches and equally responsible to the three national offices. I accepted the job since I was convinced the ecumenical approach was the only sensible route and urged that other denominations be invited to participate. The press made much of the fact that this was the first appointment of this kind in Canada and also the first time a Protestant layman had been put on the payroll of the Roman Catholic Church.

I returned to Toronto in August of that year. At the same time "Theologo '67" was being held as a centennial event at St. Michael's College. Leading theologians from all over the world were in attendance and media coverage was extensive. A dinner was arranged to enable the church press to hear Dr. Albert Vandenheuvel, Director of Communications for the World Council of Churches. It was also used as an opportunity for me to be introduced to the church hierarchy who had recently hired me and for me to say a few words about my philosophy of religious broadcasting.

I repeated the theme that it was unethical for churches to use airtime, provided free by the broadcasting industry, for the promotion of denominational dogma. To speak on an individual basis was advertising and if they continued they should pay for their time the same as General Motors. If, on the other hand, they could agree to speak with one voice about the issues of the day and give moral direction to the concerns of society, they would find broadcasters eager to co-operate and an audience prepared to give them a hearing. I received some criticism later for my remarks concerning the uselessness of church worship broadcasts. I felt then and still do, that it is one of the most ineffectual means of communication the church employs. As it stands, they commit a double error. Unless the service is changed to fit the requirements of the broadcast media, it loses both its validity as an effective programme and as a worship service. The service itself was never meant to be broadcast and clergy who insist on it are more interested in self-aggrandizement than they are in communication.

At the end of the evening I was approached by Leo Rampen, executive producer at the CBC and the Reverend Brian Freeland, religious advisor to the CBC. They said CBC television was planning to start a new network programme the following month which would be a current affairs show dealing with religion. Would I be interested in being the programme host? "It will delve deeply into the nature of man to discover his spiritual dimension," explained Rampen. "As a matter of fact we've taken our programme title from a second century bishop, St. Iraneus, who said, 'The glory of God is in man fully alive.' The name of the series will be *Man Alive*."

Audience Response

I SEES YA
AND I LIKES YA.

*I do not believe the Canadian public
is apathetic, they just need to be touched
in some special way.*

The amount of audience mail a television series draws has always been a fairly accurate gauge of its impact, provided, of course, that the mail is not solicited on the air. A programme may be extremely popular but draw very little mail. It simply takes more time and effort to write than viewers are usually willing to invest, unless they have been particularly moved. Because of its subject matter and its method of presentation, *Man Alive* has always enjoyed a heavy mail response.

This doesn't mean the letters are always complimentary. The series and its producers have been damned regularly and I have been described at various times as "blasphemer," "communist sympathizer" and "tool of the devil."

It is sometimes surprising which elements of the programme cause letters to be written. Very often complaints have nothing to do with the actual programme content.

I was soundly taken to task once for allowing myself to be filmed drinking a glass of beer in a Maritime bar while interviewing the bartender. My attire also became a concern for the viewers. For many programmes I chose to wear a turtleneck sweater. This became a trademark of sorts and there are some viewers who are still convinced that I always wear one. Many letters have been received from people offering to buy me a shirt and tie. Others felt the turtleneck was acceptable except when interviewing a bishop or a cardinal. Then they thought decorum should take the place of comfort.

Because our subject is religion the programmes elicit their share of what I call "kook" mail. These letters are all basically the same. They begin rationally and neatly enough, but as the writer gets worked up the script becomes wilder, then illegible. Page after page is filled, including the margins, with scripture quotes and personal pronouncements. Some are briefer and more to the point. My favourite of these is one from a Saskatoon man who wrote. "Dear Mr. Bonisteel, This may come as a surprise to you, but I am the Son of God. And my father and I don't like your show."

This letter happened to arrive at breakfast and I read it at the table. My daughter, then ten, asked, "Are you going to answer that one, Dad?" I said that I would like to, but couldn't make out the street address on the letter.

"Don't worry," she assured me, "there can't be that many Jesus Christs in Saskatoon."

Since I am the visible member of the *Man Alive* team almost all the mail is addressed to me. Much of it is straightforward, commenting on the most recent programme, requesting additional information, or asking that the programme be repeated. Some letters however, pour out personal concerns and ask for comments and advice. Many viewers seem to need someone with whom to share their experiences and, for better or worse, I have been selected.

Over the years letters have arrived from parents needing help with teenage children, asking advice on sexual problems, or how to rescue their adolescents from religious cults, curbing violence in the media, or commenting on drugs, child abuse and suicide prevention. Some letters tell stories of persecution by the church or the courts or government and request that *Man Alive* take action.

Many letters are stories of hope and courage from individuals who have overcome great adversity and discovered a deeper more

33

meaningful life because of the struggle.

The vast majority of viewers who write do not want help nor do they expect their tales related on the air. They simply want to make contact.

Some letters are addressed to me to be given to people I have interviewed on the programme. It has always been our policy not to give out addresses of those we have talked to, but letters from viewers are certainly passed on. Our programme about Jocelyn, a Winnipeg girl who was bravely coping with a terminal illness, resulted in some viewers sending money and medallions they had arranged to be blessed, in order to help. I do not believe the Canadian public is apathetic, they just need to be touched in some special way.

Viewers send me manuscripts of books or articles they have written. I try and point out to them that I am not in the publishing business and cannot be of assistance. Because of our uncertain postal conditions and the bulk of mail received by the CBC, some become lost and I have had to face the fury of budding authors over the loss of their "masterpiece."

My favourite letters are those from viewers who have, as a result of our programme, decided to take some step, make a decision, right some wrong, come to a deeper understanding of what it means to be human. One of the most important contributions from viewers is the suggestion of programme ideas. At times these are stories of exceedingly limited appeal or suggested as a result of some vested interest, but quite often the ideas are sound. The Shroud of Turin is perhaps the best example. Many people wrote suggesting this as a worthwhile programme. It took a few years for it to be produced, but in the end it was an effective and extremely popular *Man Alive*.

Many people seem to think that their letters have no effect. This is decidedly not the case. An unfavourable response to a programme is looked at very carefully by both the staff and management of the CBC. If the complaint is considered valid every effort is made to rectify the problem and guarantee that it is not repeated. A favourable response is also looked at as a means of judging what the public appreciates and helps us provide more of this in the future.

Viewers' response does not always come through the post office. Often it is in person. Because of my travelling schedule I am constantly meeting *Man Alive* aficionados in airports, hotels, restaurants and on streets all over Canada. For the most part it is a pleasant 'hello,' a smile of recognition, a pat on the back.

Sometimes, however, it turns into much more.

There was the man in Edmonton who caught up with me on the street, threw his arms around me and said 'Roy! How are you. Good to see you again. I...l...My God, I've never met you before in my life." He went on to explain that I seemed so familiar he couldn't help himself. "I feel I know you better than my next door neighbour."

While his response was gratifying, I found it a bit sad that my flickering image on his television set each week seemed closer to him than his neighbour.

A nun once got flustered when she saw me in Vancouver. "I always watch your show Mr. Bonisteel, but I wish it was on earlier. Ten-thirty is very late for me. I solved the problem by having a television set put in my bedroom and I want you to know I go to bed with you every Monday night."

Suddenly she realized what she had said. "I mean you are in my bedroom every Monday night...that is...I never go to bed without you...what I mean...." Red-faced and embarrassed she turned and ran before I could tell her I knew what she meant.

A woman from St. John's, Newfoundland spotted me in a hotel lobby as I was waiting for a ride to the airport. At the moment I was about to leave she seized the opportunity, ran across the lobby, grabbed me by the arm and said in a marvellous Newfoundland accent. "I sees ya and I likes ya."

Some viewers blur your identity with other CBC hosts. A man in Toronto greeted me once with. "Hey you're Patrick Watson of *Man Alive*!"

"No," I said, "I'm Roy Bonisteel."

"Right! I never miss the *Ombudsman*!"

In Barrie once a fellow approached me in a bar with, "Well, what on earth are you doing here?" I explained I had been attending a clergy conference involved in training priests for radio broadcasting.

"I didn't know you did that sort of thing," he exclaimed. He stared at me for a while then asked, "You are Russ Jackson the quarter-back aren't you?"

After several encounters like this in one day you tend to become flippant, particularly after many hours of travel. If someone asks, "You wouldn't be Roy Bonisteel would you?" You answer, "Not if I could help it!" When they thrust a piece of paper in your hand as you are rushing for an appointment you sign "Gordon Sinclair," or "The Friendly Giant." But most attempts at humour backfire.

Once, flying out of Montreal, a man spotted me as he was settling into his seat a few rows ahead.

"Aren't you Roy Bonisteel?" he demanded.

"No" I replied, "I'm much better looking than he is!"

"You certainly are not," he shouted, and buckled himself in.

At the termination of the flight I decided to apologize and as I made my way down the aisle, I paused at his seat and said, "I'm sorry I said that. I am Roy Bonisteel."

He gave me a withering look and sneered, "Like hell you are. You'll never be half the man he is!"

My favourite incident happened during a flight out of Toronto when I was accompanied by one of my producers. After several encounters with appreciative viewers at the terminal he said, "Roy, if any really nice looking girls recognize you, I hope you'll introduce me!" As soon as we were airborne a very pretty Air Canada hostess approached me. She said, "You're Roy Bonisteel aren't you?"

"Yes I am," I replied. Out of the corner of my eye I could see my producer waiting for the magic moment.

"I'm sure you won't remember me," said the stewardess, "but you taught me in Sunday School in St. Catharines fifteen years ago." I noticed my producer slump in his seat, then collapse even further when she asked, "What are you doing now?"

In press interviews and radio talk shows I am often asked if instant recognition is a problem for me. To be honest I do not like being awakened on planes or buses to be told who I am. Neither do I enjoy the person who sits and stares, and stares, and stares, as though waiting for me to do something strange.

Once I sat in the Halifax airport trying to hide behind the *Gazette*, while a man in a phone booth kept saying, "Yes, it's him. He's sitting just six feet away. He's reading the newspaper. Really it's him. I can tell by his hair."

For the most part I consider it a compliment when people say hello. If television viewers in this country think enough of *Man Alive* to turn on their sets and watch, surely the least I can do is pay them the courtesy of returning the compliment.

To be invited into the living rooms of a million people every week is a very gratifying, yet humbling experience. I try never to take it lightly.

Malcolm Muggeridge

THIS PROGRAMME COMES TO YOU BY COURTESY OF LUCIFER INC.

*No television. I've had my aerials
removed. You don't miss it at all, and it
is a necessary operation.*

For years Malcolm Muggeridge has been telling anyone who would listen that the world is "going to hell in a hand basket." This purveyor of doom and gloom comes down particularly hard on television calling it a "tool of the devil." The irony here is that this man's shock of snowy hair, glittering blue eyes, and pixyish expression make up one of the best known faces in the world because of the television set. Muggeridge maintains that television is barely removed from pornography. He feels pornography is a "sickness of the soul and part of our national death wish." He says we have disassociated eroticism from procreation and, because of our over-indulgence, will inevitably lose our sexual appetite. The entire trend, he says, is toward impotence.

Next on his list is government. He says the future of England and the United States is extremely uncertain and adds, almost as an afterthought, that Western Europe is on the verge of collapse, while France and Italy have already fallen by virtue of a communist takeover in the guise of democracy.

Then the churches. Here Muggeridge sputters and fumes with indignant rage. He claims the mainline churches have "played around with their liturgies" so much, in order to become more attractive, they have lost their sense of permanence. He says he feels sorry for the Anglican and Roman Catholic churches because they have moved so far into the social gospel.

When I first interviewed Muggeridge in 1968, one year after *Man Alive* began, the ecumenical movement was very strong in Canada. A plan of union had been drawn up by the Anglican and United Churches and other denominations were talking merger. I mentioned this to Malcolm. He snorted contemptuously. "It will never work. They are reacting out of desperation. It is exactly like a group of drunks reeling out of a saloon. They have to hold on to each other to stand up."

He has little love for organized religion, yet admits that if he were going to join any church he would be a Roman Catholic, which, for him, has the history, the form and the romance he craves. However, he is quick to add, "I would not make a good church member. You remember Groucho Marx saying he wouldn't want to be a member of a club that would have him as a member? Well, I wouldn't want to join a church that would accept me."

These are his favourite topics, but almost any subject will start him into animated oratory.

Muggeridge in full rhetorical flight is a sight to behold in person, yet even better on film. He is one of those who the camera seems to gild with a certain sparkle that enhances an already flawless performance. He loves the camera and the camera appears to love him back.

Muggeridge seems to choreograph his every on-camera appearance. His movements punctuate and underline the main points so as to create an emotional atmosphere contagious to the viewer. This was particularly evident in one of his discourses on television.

"Let me tell you this," (eyes boring straight ahead, chin raised and thrust outward) "from close acquaintance and after much thought, that television has become the devil's favourite instrument" (eyes wide with fright, body pulls away from camera in shock). "People ask me how it is that feeling about television as I do, I still occasionally appear" (voice quizzical, chummy posture, smile begins). "Well, I see myself as a man playing piano in a brothel" (smile widens) "who includes in his repertoire 'Abide With Me' (eyes roll Heavenward, smile still wider) "in the hope of elevating both the clients and the staff" (eyes crinkle shut as face breaks into hearty chuckle).

His brothel remark was first made on that 1968 programme. I have heard him repeat it many times since, from the platform, on the air, and in print. It is one of a wide range of anecdotes, epigrams, one-liners and eloquent repartee that he keeps at the ready and uses with devastating effect.

I will always remember that first interview for another comment he made. This was off-camera. I was relatively new to television and its intricacies, also somewhat in awe of a person of Muggeridge's stature. We taped about forty minutes when a break was called and a set change made. Malcolm and I took advantage of this time to get our make-up repaired before the next session. The producer called me aside and said, "It's going fine Roy but I want you to change your approach. Up to now you've let him have his way. Now really challenge him." As we walked back to the studio Malcolm asked, "Well, did they tell you to go for my jugular?"

"Yes they did," I answered in surprise.

"Well, let me tell you something I've learned in my many years in television. You have to be true to yourself. You can't pretend to be what you're not. If you are a phony that camera will find you out. Honesty always eventually shows through."

I have never forgotten his advice and every time I have interviewed him since I have been struck by his basic integrity and honesty. No matter how much we have disagreed and argued, no matter how angry viewers have reacted to some of his statements, he has never wavered from a fundamental position of seeing the world in black and white, with evil gradually and inexorably winning.

Malcolm Muggeridge was born in 1903. After a stint as a lecturer at the University of Cairo, he plunged into journalism, writing for a number of British and foreign papers. He became internationally known as editor of *Punch* magazine, a position he held during the fifties and, of course, through his many appearances on British television and radio. A succession of pithy and provocative books, *Tread Softly For You Tread On My Jokes, The Thirties, Muggeridge Through The Microphone* then, in 1969, *Jesus Rediscovered*, introduced millions to his uniquely incisive mind.

When not writing books, or appearing on television he lectures in various countries and contributes pungent articles to the world press.

When I visited him at his home in 1978 he was working on a piece for *The New York Times*. "They have asked me to write an article listing twenty-five conclusions I have arrived at in my lifetime," he said. "They apparently assume I reach a conclusion every three years."

He lives near Robertsbridge, a small village about sixty kilometres southeast of London, England, in a fine old country home with his wife Kitty, a most devoted woman and a charming hostess.

In a small, thatched coach house adjacent to the main house Malcolm was the perfect country squire poking a wood fire in a rather smoky fireplace and offering sherry all around.

"None for me," he said with a smile of self satisfaction after everyone else's glasses were brimming. "I've been an abstainer for twelve years. I neither drink nor smoke now, although I used to do both. One time during an interview with America's Edward R. Murrow, who as you know was an inveterate chain smoker, the show had to be halted because we had both disappeared from view in a cloud of smoke."

Muggeridge is a great story teller and his anecdotes of his experiences over the years with people as diverse as Bertrand Russell and Hugh Hefner assure a rapt audience.

I saw another side of Malcolm that evening — the doting grandpa. His son, daughter-in-law and family arrived unexpectedly, but no worry as there was always room for extra guests and both Kitty and Malcolm were radiant with joy as they played with the children.

"I fear for the children today," he told me later. "It's this medium we work in. Networks are naive if they think by late scheduling they can keep children from watching the pornography and the violence on the tube."

"How do you handle it when your grandchildren arrive?" I asked.

"Very simply. No television. I've had my aerials removed. It's not such a painful procedure. It's much like having your prostate gland taken out. You don't miss it at all, and it is a necessary operation."

The next morning in a studio in London, we continued our discussion of television for the *Man Alive* cameras.

"Why do you insist that television is so evil?" I asked.

"Basically because it presents the world in terms of fantasy rather than reality. It makes man feel that life is a thing to look at. He's spending four to five hours a day looking into a screen.

40

That's a good slice of his life. The drama is taking place there on the screen and he sits there inertly looking at it."

"But you're not giving the viewer much credit," I insisted. "Surely he can look at the screen and say I realize that is fantasy. That's not happening."

"Come now. You've been appearing on television a lot. Would you say that the great bulk of viewers are looking at it as fantasy and not taking it seriously?"

"There are programmes I want them to take seriously such as mine," I countered. "I'm not trying to fool the public. I am showing them you right now. I want them to see the real Malcolm Muggeridge. Is that not possible?"

"Absolutely impossible, because they are seeing me and they are seeing you as images, not as real men. Before I had my aerials removed one of the effects television used to have on my wife and I was putting us to sleep. One time we dropped off and I had the most macabre experience of suddenly waking up and saying who the hell is that on the screen? And it was me. Even appearing on television makes one person, two people."

Muggeridge went on to list the evils he saw in the medium of television. He was alarmed by what he called the increase in pornography, especially in American programmes and the vast amounts of money spent in prime time to sell useless products. He also attacked the editing of material in news programmes to fit pre-ordained time requirements. This, he maintains, leads to distortion as many items require in-depth reporting.

I assured him that there were responsible people in the television industry fighting for honesty and truthful reporting. I reminded him of his American colleague Edward R. Murrow who won such great respect both from the viewers and the industry.

"Well," he answered, "Ed was a friend of mine and I did a lot of television work with him. But even Ed got caught up in the fantasy of television. He became an image more than a man toward the end of his life. And, for that reason, with all the fame and success he rightly had, there was a melancholy about him and though he became this great figure in television, this man of integrity and great pundit, I think in a way it killed him."

"His mantle has now been placed on Walter Cronkite," I said.

"And that is a wonderful irony. Ed was a very serious, solemn person who took enormous trouble over programmes, but I think Cronkite is a kind of a joke figure."

"I guess his closing line to his newscasts must give you a

chuckle," I said. "That's the way it is!"

"Wonderful! Absolutely wonderful! The BBC does the same thing, 'And that's the world this weekend!' You listen to four or five assorted items and you think of the world and the universe and its history and its God and its destiny and that's really the world this weekend, not these five little tenth rate bits of reporting. But, there it is!"

"If we were to believe what you say about the evils of television and follow your example by taking our aerials down we would miss so much that is good. It might be no loss if the viewers didn't see me, but it would be if they didn't see Malcolm Muggeridge, or Mother Teresa of Jean Vanier or Anthony Bloom."

"I quite agree with you that there are exceptional things that can be done and certainly the Mother Teresa programme was one of them and I cherish having had the honour of taking part in particular programmes which I know have brought people to see reality a little bit. But, television is still a fraudulent channel of communication. It can, as you say, occasionally be effective but the distortion is terrible and the distortion in many ways is worse in relation to really serious, highly regarded programmes; programmes such as Clark's *Civilization* or Bronowski's *Ascent of Man*. Now Clark, who is a friend of mine and whom I like very much describes civilization virtually without mentioning the Christian religion — quite a singular omission. People seeing that programme, prepared by a very cultivated man, miss this central point."

I told him I agreed with much that he said particularly the manipulation of the viewer by the advertiser and the rating obsessed programmer, but his statements that "all television lies" and "the camera always lies" I found hard to swallow.

"You make it seem like the people behind the cameras, the producers, the editors, the writers, are all part of some evil plot and I don't think that is true" I said.

"Not for a single moment," he answered, "but it is a deception operation, not because of those who operate it or those of us who appear on it, but it is the facts of translating a living scene into an image and believing that the image is reality that causes this distortion and that is what the camera does."

"Well what are we to do then?" I asked. "Should we tear down our aerials as you have done? And what about those of us in the medium, should we leave and throw stones at it the way you do or stay in it and try to change it?"

"I think everyone has to work it out inside his own conscience. My own opinion is a pessimistic one. I believe that a Christian today is in the same position as Christians in the early church, that is, they will be forced to detach themselves. In my own humble way I've tried to detach myself, not just in connection with television but other areas, education, government, hospitals. As we move into a post-Christian era in which the assumptions of the Christian faith are no longer valid, you will find that devout Christians will be in the same position as they are in the communist world. They will be forced to sustain their faith by separating themselves from society."

"But if you are so concerned about Christian values and introducing other people to them it seems to me that television cannot be ignored. You could reach millions of people at any given time, more than you are ever going to reach through the pulpit," I said.

"That may be, but I have a theory that this is the fourth temptation to which Jesus was subjected occuring centuries later. As you know he'd been offered previously the temptation to turn stones into bread, to abolish hunger, then to jump off the top of the temple without coming to harm thereby achieving celebrity status and to accept the kingdom of heaven on earth, all of which he turned down flat.

"The fourth temptation is an offer from a big tycoon who says 'Look you've got this wonderful material, this gospel, this good news to bring to mankind, why waste your time with a few people? I'll put you on the air in prime time so you can reach everybody. Now you can say what you like. There's not going to be any vulgar advertising. Just at the end of your discourse in very discreet language we'll put: this programme comes to you by courtesy of Lucifer Inc.' "

Almost every discussion with Muggeridge eventually gets around to his Christian view of life. For him the Christian position is a bright beam illuminating all perceptions of the modern world.

When I talked to him again in 1979 we were preparing a programme on the sacredness of life. We didn't have to travel far to meet him this time since he was lecturing at the University of Western Ontario in London, Ontario.

It was good to see the Muggeridges again. We chatted over a light lunch Kitty had prepared of cheese, bread, fruit and yogurt, (Malcolm eats no meat) and then settled down in front of the camera for another *Man Alive* session.

He told me he had recently interviewed a man on British television who had murdered his wife at her request.

"He told me she had been desperately ill and in pain and asked him to do it, so he did. In talking to him about it he mentioned he was an atheist so I told him I didn't see why an atheist shouldn't murder his wife if she asks him to, because the argument for respecting life rests in my opinion on a belief in a creator whose creation is an act of love."

"Are you saying then," I asked, "that it's an individual thing? Life may be sacred to me if I'm a believer, but for a person who isn't, it doesn't really matter?"

"I can't see any basis in which a person could regard life as sacred if he sees it merely as a part of an animal set-up. For me life is something that deserves our infinite respect and we are not in a position under any circumstances to judge its quality or necessity. Life is sacred because it is created by God for a purpose and that purpose comes to an end when you die. It's not for you to choose the moment at which to die. It's not for you to say I don't want to live because it's not your notion that's being worked out. It's part of the purpose of the creator and that alone makes it your duty to live out your life. At the same time, of course, as I feel myself at seventy-five having few more years to live, I'm glad to say, I feel enormously looking forward to this end."

"But if life is so sacred and precious why are you looking forward to death?" I asked.

"Because what makes it sacred is not just what it is, but its potentiality. If I thought my existence here was the whole story, I wouldn't find it sacred at all. I would think it a rather trivial thing and that the moment one wearied of it one would be perfectly entitled to bump oneself off. It's only because you see it in a setting of a divine creation which partakes of eternity as well as time that it's sacred."

"So for the Christian who believes in an after-life, death holds no sting?"

"That's right. But I'm not happy with the word after-life because that implies another life like this life. I prefer to see it as a projection of life from time into eternity."

"And this is desirable...."

"Infinitely so."

"If eternity is so desirable why don't we move into it at age twenty or forty? Why do we wait so long?"

"Because that would be trying to intervene on one's own behalf in God's purpose and that is what twentieth century man is trying to do all the time. He is trying to introduce his will into God's and that's why he's making such a mess of it. If I say to you, 'Yes, I look forward to the time when my life will partake of eternity instead of time, therefore cut my throat and let me go quickly,' you wouldn't do it. If a boy at school was looking forward to his holidays and therefore thought it appropriate to run away from school before his term was over, you wouldn't applaud that.''

''What does the sacredness of life tell us about some of the current social problems that we face, abortion for example?''

''My view of abortion is that it's the most evil and wicked thing that's happened for a long time. Here is a creature, conceived, existing with all the potentialities of a human being to participate in God's purpose as a human being. It might turn out to be a Beethoven. It might turn out to be a village idiot. It might turn out to be anything, but God has created it. It exists. Then we come along with our little piffling purposes and our little emotions about population and one thing or another and say we're going to kill it. We're not going to let it exist. Mankind is going to have to suffer for having done that. This notion of using our will to destroy a creature before it's even born is something that is abhorrent and is practiced very widely, to the point when last year I think there were fifty million abortions. Incidently, I've thought about the idiocy of this whole thing. You have on the one hand fifty million abortions and on the other the whole human race apparently spellbound by the incubation of a baby in a test tube. You know, when I was editor of *Punch* we used to try to think of things like that to make a good cartoon, but you couldn't invent that — fifty million babies killed and everybody awed, enchanted by the fact that a sperm has fertilized in a test tube.''

''Some people would say that it's the quality of life that matters, that it's better to end that life before it's begun rather than have it born into a home where it's not wanted or loved.'' I said.

''But who's deciding this policy? On what basis can a person choose about a baby before it's born that it's better unborn? One of the things that befalls people, when they try to exist with only the concept of man and nothing higher than man, is the terrible arrogance that overtakes them because they have to believe that man is terribly important because that's all there is in the universe.''

''What do you say then about the person who is driven to

45

suicide?''

"I feel desperately sorry for them. I've been driven to the point of suicide myself as a matter of fact. It's a thing that can happen, because we can all fall down. But nothing would convince me that it was right. As a Christian I am convinced that it is right that we should live out this little drama in which God has involved us. The termination of it lies with him and not with us.''

"It sounds like you're saying that Christians never commit suicide because they believe in a creator.''

"But Christians do commit suicide.''

"Of course they do.''

"But they commit a sin. That's the difference. They kill themselves because they can't continue life any more, but they are aware of sinning if they're Christians. You may remember when Solzhenitsyn came over here he said, 'You may find reports of me having committed suicide, but I could never commit suicide because I am a Christian and it would be a sin.' But of course, particularly as one grows old, the termination of life seems infinitely desirable. One longs for the end of it like one longs for the end of a tedious voyage. You've had three weeks. You've got another three days to go and those three days seem almost longer than the three weeks because it's a wonderful release, out of time, out of flesh, away from this awful ego that pulls one down. That's a Christian view.''

"Where do you stand on capital punishment?''

"I think that it's a horrible thing and something that brings out the very worst in people and only dubiously solves any of the difficulties of crime. On the other hand, I believe that there are possible situations in which the evil of capital punishment is less than the evil with which it can cope, as in war.''

"There are other decisions our society has to make. Euthanasia, for example, an action often taken by the family or the doctor. How do you feel about that?''

"As a Christian I do not consider that anyone's entitled to make that decision.''

"If you were a doctor you couldn't do it either?''

"I wouldn't ever do it, nor would, I think, any Christian doctor that I know. It wouldn't necessarily follow that he would consider the most appropriate treatment, for the patient that he was attending with love and care, would be to project his days for the longest time. He would make that judgment as a Christian in what was the best interest of the patient in Christian terms. But he would never have the arrogance to say, in conjunction with some committee or the family, that this person's life should now be cut short. That would be a piece of arrogance quite impermissible unless he believes there's no creator. Then you treat human beings as livestock. That's how they're increasingly being treated. Western man is turning away from God to such an extent he will come to feel himself and to feel his fellow man are animals. And in a factory farm situation, if there's one who's in poor physical state, you kill it. You will live to see governments getting rid of the terrible burdens of the senile old, mental defective or people like that by the simple expedient of killing them. The only government that's ever done that was the Nazi government. That's the reason euthanasia has been delayed for thirty years, because it was in fact one of the war crimes charged against the Nazis at Nurenberg. So for the *Guiness Book of Records* we can say that it takes thirty years in a democratic society to transform a war crime into an act of compassion — just thirty years.

"I often symbolize in my mind the old puzzle. You've got a raft with two people in it and it can only hold one and one of the people is Bernard Shaw and the other is an imbecile. Who should jump in the water? The materialist would always say of course the imbecile should be pushed into the water and we'll keep Shaw to write more plays. I think the Christian view is exactly the opposite. If anybody has enough love for mankind to take a header himself even though the other person is, in social terms, worthless, that achieves more for the human race than any play that anyone could write or any thing they could do. It's very difficult and I recognize the difficulty, but I simply insist that at the end of the day the only thing that will work is that the people judging have this sense of something greater than man to whom they can refer the question rather than considering it in terms of social utility or intellectual or physical capacity."

"But in a democratic society we have to live by laws and we now have laws being made on abortion and euthanasia. Could Malcolm Muggeridge tell us how we can get humane laws?"

" For an inhumane purpose you will never get a humane law. The abortion law that was passed in England was full of safeguards to make it humane. Within a month all those safeguards were inoperative and they are still. In other words, it simply was abortion on demand. Similarly if you have a euthanasia bill within a month it will mean that anyone who any doctor or local authority thinks should be got rid of can be got rid of, because you can't make a humane law out of inhumane assumptions and unless you've got the humility and Christian love to recognize that, you can't apply humane standards to this question."

After our interview was concluded and our goodbyes had been said I thought how much about Malcolm was unchanged in the eleven years since we had first met. Age was slowing his step and stooping his shoulders, his snowy hair was thinner and more wispy, but his mind was as sharp and his tongue as devastatingly eloquent as ever. His view of the downward spiral of society and its only chance for survival remained the same.

Viewers' reaction to Muggeridge is always predictable. They hear what they want to hear and consequently agree with him wholeheartedly, disagree with him vehemently or are simply delighted by his ability to turn a phrase.

The fact is Malcolm Muggeridge is unique. In a world of fence sitting and compromise he is immovable. His critics are legion because he will not bend to popular whim or man made morality. His pragmatic stand is called old fashioned, stuffy, pompous, self righteous by those who do not see the world in such black and white terms. But no one can deny the steadfastness of his views or his genius in promulgating them.

He does not proselytize in the evangelical sense. He is not interested in gathering converts to his side. He prefers to observe and comment from a loftier position, apart from any organized cause.

To know him is to discover a man with great compassion and generosity. If the day were to come when, God forbid, all his dire predictions come true, I can't even imagine him saying "I told you so."

Elie Wiesel

THE WITNESS

*Silence to me is the soul of the word. It is
what cannot be said that is important.*

"Let me tell you a story," Elie Wiesel said softly and so began a
Man Alive interview I will always remember for its sensitivity and
passion. Elie Wiesel speaks in "stories" about the Holocaust,
about Jews and about hope in a hopeless world.

He has been called "the spiritual archivist of the Holocaust"
and "the messenger of the Jewish dead to the living." Author
of over a dozen books, recipient of many awards and degrees for
his insightful prose, Wiesel told me, "I am just a storyteller, only
a witness."

In the spring of 1944, fifteen year old Wiesel, his parents and
three sisters were placed on a cattle train and sent to Auschwitz.
He saw the Nazis kill his father. His mother and youngest sister
also died there. Wiesel escaped the ovens by lying about his age
on the advice of a fellow prisoner. Thinking he was eighteen, he
was sent as a slave labourer to Buchenwald.

His book *Night* is an autobiographical account of a boy witnessing the horrors of Auschwitz and Buchenwald. His words are powered by the emotion and impact of this experience and by the added guilt he deeply feels by surviving when millions did not.

English is Wiesel's second language. His style is haunting and poetic, but rarely grammatically correct. What we hear are thoughts, painful and unrelenting, linked only by his desire for us to understand the turmoil of his experience.

During our interview I quoted a sentence from his book. "Have we ever thought of the horror of the death of God in the soul of a child who is suddenly confronted with absolute evil?" Had God died in his soul?

His dark eyes became sad and seemed to sink even deeper beneath his wide pale brow as he answered, "Let me tell you a story. When I was a child I gave God absolute faith. I gave him my childhood. I was very much shaken and crushed by the desertion of God, more than by the desertion of man. I didn't expect much from man, but I expected everything from God. The tragedy of the believer is much worse than the tragedy of the non-believer you know. I had the worst moment of fear in my entire existence. It came that first night when I arrived into the "Kingdom of Night" which I have tried to describe in my book. I was still a child and I still had God in me. I still knew how to pray. I didn't know what was going on. In 1944 everybody knew except us. We didn't know what was happening. We didn't know what it meant, Auschwitz. No one could tell us. I remember it was night and as we walked away from the train people were screaming and shouting all around us. And the fire. We suddenly saw the fire. And Jews coming from all over. Marching. Converging on one point. So many Jews, coming from so many countries, so many tongues. They were so different. The young and the old, dark and blonde, silent and talkative, afraid and courageous. Suddenly I had the feeling that this was it. The Messiah had come, and I had a part in it. Together with my friends we had tried to bring the Messiah and now we had succeeded. He was here.

The moment of fear came when I realized it was the wrong Messiah. It was the anti-Messiah.

I asked Wiesel if this was the moment when, as he had written, "Satan took over the world."

"It was worse than Satan. Some madness or madman took over the world. Something happened and we don't really know

50

what. I can't even describe it to you. I can say it in a whisper. I can sing it in a song, but it would be a lamentation. But to actually say what happened, I don't know. It was something that will lay on our conscience for all time to come. I think it was the greatest event in history, but it was a transitory event and that is the tragedy. That is the guilt feeling of the storyteller. He cannot even tell the tale, except to say it was an eclipse of God.''

I reminded him that in his book he asserted that he had then felt "stronger than God.''

"Yes, it was a very curious feeling we had, those of us who survived. All the gods and godesses were against us and they tried to kill us. They succeeded, of course, in such large numbers, but somehow they did not succeed in killing all of us. We became invincible. At least for the moment, we became immortal. At that moment of awareness, we felt stronger than God. If we ever had a reason to say 'no' to God, or feel purer than God, more righteous or more indestructible, it was at that moment.''

But what was the price of that survival? In *Night* Wiesel recounts an incident where his father is struck by his Nazi captors. Wiesel watched this happening and in his words "never raised an eyelid.''

"What was happening to you at that time?'' I asked.

"The worst thing they did to us,'' he replied, "was not really to kill us, but to have us exposed to the things that are in Jews which make us survive. When I think of this whole period it makes me sad because I know, despite our bravado, despite our optimism, we have inside something very profound. We have an insight into something that can drive us mad. It was the first time I realized what I am capable of. It was really that scene when I saw what they did to my father and I did nothing. I did not jump on the aggressor. I saw then that man is not as good as he wants to be. Man is not God. Man is not even human.''

I was interested in Wiesel's opinion on the power of prayer. He had written that, as he approached the furnace at Auschwitz, he had not wanted to pray but despite himself he had prayed. The words just came. I asked him if he prayed today and if so how. There was a long silence. I wondered if he had heard the question. Then finally, softly and almost apologetically he answered.

"Forgive me. I cannot answer you that. It's very personal and I'm afraid to trespass. But I can tell you that I need prayer very much. The form is different today. I would call it singing. I would call it defiance. Sometimes one of my characters in one of my tales turns to God and says, 'I know what you want. You want

51

me to stop praying and therefore I shall pray.' "

I inquired about those who upon arrival at Auschwitz did not have his strong faith.

"The first inmates to yield to the system and become collaborators and help the Germans were the humanists, the professors of literature, the artists, the painters, the writers. Suddenly they lost touch with something solid, with something absolute and they, out of despair or resignation, immediately gave up. On the other hand, priests resisted well. There were very few priests among the sadists, but the rabbis resisted better than anyone else. There was not one single rabbi who collaborated with the Germans. There were thousands and thousands of rabbis in my region. Any one of them could have made a deal or a pact with the Germans. But first the Germans would have had to corrupt them. It was a spiritual battle between two systems. Not one single rabbi betrayed, yet I know personally of hundreds who went to their death rather than betray. I understand why many who came without faith got their faith there, and many who came with faith lost it there too. It's the same thing."

Wiesel spoke with a soft, well modulated, almost whispered delivery, but there was anger mixed with pain as he remembered. His quiet condemnation of other countries that had not helped, and Christians who turned their backs, was devastating. He claimed that as early as 1942 leaders and public officials in England, Sweden, Switzerland and America knew exactly what Auschwitz meant. The only ones who didn't know what was going on were the Jews in the occupied countries, in his case Hungary. In March and April 1944, when he and his neighbours were taken to Auschwitz, they thought it was just a peaceful railway station somewhere in Poland. They could not even imagine that thousands of men, women and children could be massacred and reduced to ash and the world would keep silent.

"Why didn't more Christians come to the aid of the Jews?" I asked.

"I have no answer," he replied, "no real answer. I don't understand what happened to them during the war. I guess God kept silent. It's easy for me to become an accuser of Christianity. It's almost too easy. And Christians themselves, those who are honest and sincere, understand that the crisis taking place now within Christianity is very profound because, it's a terrible thing to say, but Christianity failed. Christianity knew its bankruptcy at Auschwitz. You see, Auschwitz did not take place in a vacuum. It took place within a given setting, a social, philosophical and geological setting. A setting of 2,000 years of Christianity.''

This was the point in the interview that received the most criticism when the programme went on the air. A number of viewers, and some members of the *Man Alive* staff, thought I should have objected more strenuously to his condemnation of the Christian response during the holocaust. I chose a different tack.

"I'm not going to defend Christianity at this point," I said, "but isn't it possible that it wasn't Christianity that died there? Mightn't it have been only a concept of Christianity that was not big enough to encompass this evil?"

"No doubt," he answered. "Pope John XXIII felt that, but he also felt guilt. I believe Christianity did die at Auschwitz. Certainly Judaism didn't. We came out of it dead, but alive. We lost millions, but Judaism came out of it unharmed, untarnished. I know people who observed Shabbat in Auschwitz. I know a starving rabbi who would not eat meat in Auschwitz. I know of a train load of Jews rejoicing at Auschwitz, singing of glory, dancing and blessing the Torah. In a curious and grotesque way they were right because Judaism did not lose face. It withstood Auschwitz. Christianity did not.''

"You mention Pope John. You say he felt guilty. I'm wondering if feeling guilty is enough to keep it from happening again?"

"No, it is not enough. There has to be an act of repentance,'' he said. "I confess my guilt that I remained alive.''

"How about your Christian friends? Do they tell you they feel guilty? Do they confess their guilt to you?"

"I think they feel guilty," he answered. "They don't confess it, but I feel it in them. I am really pleased that both Catholics and Protestants read my books. They read them more than Jews. I respect them very much if they respect me as a Jew. I do not want to make them Jewish and I hope they don't want to make me Christian. I try to make them more Christian simply by being more Jewish. I tell them my tales and I listen to theirs. Both must have a deep concern for humanity as the basis, otherwise it is useless.''

I suggested that this deep concern for humanity and respect for human life was indeed shared by both the Christian and Jewish faith, and that there were many common elements in both religions.

"I don't agree with you on that," he replied. "I don't think we have that much in common. Theologically we have things in common, monotheism and so forth, but in practice it is not one religion with two branches, not at all. I'll give you an example.

The idea of original sin is Christian not Jewish. A Jew is born innocent and is guilty only if he becomes so, while a Christian has to constantly fight guilt. Then there is our attitude toward suffering. We don't believe in suffering. We believe that suffering is bad for human beings. We believe that suffering does not lead to salvation nor confer privilege upon anyone. To surmount suffering and to surmount the bitterness resulting from it, that may lead to privilege. And also, our relationship towards death. Death to us is something very personal and private, while in Christianity, because of its beginnings, death became part of the decorum. During the war the entire world seemed to become Christian as part of the decorum. It didn't matter much whether people died in war time. Just as it doesn't matter now in Pakistan or in Vietnam that people die. To us death is something very sacred and very personal. No, I don't see that our religion is one, but because we are so very different there are bridges possible and we can construct them, provided first we tell the truth to each other."

Elie Wiesel was one of the first persons I encountered at that time who had such profound feelings about silence. In his book, *Night* the notion of silence plays an important role. Characters in his novels assume silence for long periods. I asked him to explain what silence meant to him.

"Silence to me is the soul of the word. It is what cannot be said that is important. The words that I don't say carry weight. In my case it has to do with my childhood. I studied mysticism and grew up in this mystical climate where silence is so important. We believe that the word, the pure word, the true word, is the word of silence. Only God creates that language. We believe there were two traditions handed down at Mount Sinai. One was the oral one and the other the esoteric, the silent one. This is the silence that I try to put into my work, the silence that is linked to Sinai. There is a healthy silence, Sinai, and an unhealthy silence, the deluge or the chaos before the creation. There is a political silence which is criminal. To be silent when so many injustices are being performed is a crime. We are silent today about the wrong things. In many ways we are the most talkative generation there has ever been in the world. We were never so obsessed with communication. How many newspapers? How many radio stations? People talk, talk, talk, talk and say nothing. When we went to the moon I remember how disappointed I was. I expected something! After all! After all! Such an experience! And we expect of the man who comes to the moon to say something of eternal value, at least something poetic. What do we hear? Banal, simple words. Yet the silence still prevails. There is a universe of silence. And you can say about it what you can say about life and about death and God. And all of what you say will not make up completely what there is to be said about it."

In much of his writings Wiesel describes himself as a witness. I wondered how much frustration he felt in trying to fulfill that role.

"I feel terribly frustrated, because the tale that I try to tell, perhaps cannot be told. At one point I even doubted if it should be told. Perhaps it's a private image. Perhaps if, in 1945, all the survivors, all of them, could have taken a vow not to speak about it, not one single word, there would have been so much silence it might have changed the world. I waited ten years. Then I wrote *Night*. Perhaps if we had all done the same thing, and waited, not for ten years but forever, it might have achieved more. But I am not a philosopher. I am a witness and a messenger. And he who listens to a witness becomes in turn a witness and a messenger."

Wiesel was liberated from Buchenwald by American troops and along with four hundred other orphans boarded a train for Belgium. The train was rerouted to France on the orders of Charles de Gaulle and Wiesel ended up in Normandy. He quickly learned French, moved to Paris and began studying at the Sorbonne, supporting himself by teaching the Bible. In 1948 he went to Palestine to report on Israeli independence for a French newspaper. He later became chief correspondent for a Tel Aviv daily which assigned him to cover the United Nations in New York.

While crossing Time Square he was struck by a taxi cab and while recovering in a New York hospital decided to make America his home. This incident also became the basis for his book *The Accident*, published in 1962, which tells of a young Jewish reporter who, while hovering between life and death, reviews his life and faces the guilt he feels about his concentration camp ordeal.

I was on assignment in Europe when the *Man Alive* interview was arranged. Because of an airline strike in Canada I flew directly to New York where we were to use a studio of the educational television station. Research material was to be waiting for me when I arrived, but had been lost somewhere on a bus from Buffalo. I had to depend on my memory of his book *Night* which was really all I knew of him. We met for only a few minutes before the cameras rolled, but I was immediately impressed by the gentle warmth of this spare, sad eyed "witness."

"I really see myself as a witness," he told me. "I bear witness to the past through tales and story telling. I try to reach out, especially to the young and say 'look what happened. Listen.' It's not that awful. It's not to be sad about. It's a privilege and a curse at the same time. To live today is to remember. So listen to my tales and spread them.''

THE DIVINE
DISSENTERS

We could not, so help us God, do otherwise.
For we are sick at heart; our hearts
give us no rest for thinking of the
Land of Burning Children.

Father Daniel Berrigan, a Jesuit priest, has been credited with
doing more than any other single American in shaping attitudes
toward the long and controversial Vietnam War during the 1960's
and early 1970's. His poetry and articles, his books and lectures,
the burning of draft records at Catonsville, his trial and conviction, his underground game of hide-and-seek with the FBI, his
capture and imprisonment, all made him a figure of near-mytho-
logical dimension. He and his brother Philip, a Roman Catholic
priest of the Josephite order, became leaders of the anti-war
movement, inspiring thousands to emulate their spectacular
methods of protest. The Berrigans were idolized by the radical
left, hated by the American government and were alternately
the embarrassment and the pride of the Roman Catholic Church
in America.

My meeting with them occurred on American Thanksgiving

Day, November 1969. It had not been easy to arrange the interview. Locating the Berrigans was the main problem. They were finally tracked down at their brother Jerry's home in Syracuse, New York. It was a tense time for the two "divine dissenters," as they were popularly known. Both had recently been sentenced to jail, and while they were outwardly cheerful, it was obvious the strain of constant FBI surveillance and the impending incarceration weighed heavily on their minds. They could not have appeared more different. Philip was blonde, jovial and looked like a big, friendly bear. Daniel was slight, dark and appeared somewhat fragile. Daniel faced a three year sentence; Philip the remainder of six years. He had served only seven months before being released on his own recognizance while his case went through a series of appeals.

Philip's six year sentence aroused a storm of protest from the daily press. *The New York Times*, while pointing out that it felt his blood spilling "went beyond the bounds of legitimate protest," found the penalty excessive. It said that, while the bench had the power to fix sentences on those found guilty, it "does not have the right to impose punishment out of all proportion to the crime."

The Boston Pilot editorialized that the court was using its own means to take those it judged to be public nuisances out of circulation, and that Father Berrigan was no mortal threat to society.

The Boston Globe pointed out that pacifism was not so heinous a crime as to warrant the casual lopping off of six years of a man's life. It said "convicted thugs and murderers have been treated more gently."

When I asked Philip about going to jail, he thought it might be beneficial. "The whole peace movement needs catalyctic action from many sources. It needs a catalyst of risk, of price-paying, of suffering. Certain people have to pay up, and jail is part of it for us."

Daniel said he had mixed emotions. "I'm unhappy about the idea that jail should be the real issue when it's the horror of the war and the improbability of ending it that's at stake. I don't know what our going to jail will contribute to all of that. On the other hand, being out doesn't seem to help much."

Both said their concern about the Vietnam War had begun about 1964. "The development of our concern paralleled each other," said Philip. "We tried the demonstration route. We were in contact with political figures in Washington. We wrote letters and went through the whole liberal gamut of dissent. We found this was to no avail and came to the conclusion that civil disobedience was more and more imperative.''

Dan added, ''We also shared a great deal of mutual trouble with the church. In the last four years we've been tossed back and forth by the church like a game of ping-pong. In 1965 Phil was teaching in a seminary in Hubert, New York and was given the boot for his activities up there. Then I had no sooner settled in Baltimore than they kicked me out.''

''What kind of activities?'' I asked.

Philip answered, ''We began to organize against the Vietnam War and we did several pallid things like having panels, pro and con, on the war, a couple of peace marches and we did some writing and interviews. Pressure was brought to bear on the church authorities in New York City and from there on our society headquarters in Baltimore, so I was moved.''

''In my case,'' said Daniel, ''I was helping with the formation of a clergy-layman group against the war. This was in New York and this activity became a little bit too hot for Cardinal Spellman, who was living then, so I was given a one-way ticket to Latin America.''

Sending Daniel to Latin America was not an effective move on the part of the church hierarchy, at least if their intention was to silence him. As one friend said, ''It was like throwing Br'er Rabbit into the briar patch.'' Seeing the poverty and injustice there only deepened his radical stance. A nationwide protest against sending him to Latin America by his Jesuit brothers and other supporters had Daniel back in the United States after seven months.

Philip's transfer was ineffective as well. He joined other Catholic and Protestant groups to picket and pray at the homes of Dean Rusk and Robert McNamara.

In October 1967 Philip and three other Vietnam War protestors entered the Customs House in Baltimore and poured a mixture of their own and duck's blood into draft record files in the city's Selective Service headquarters. A great deal of discussion preceded the decision to pour blood on the records instead of just burning them. Several meetings were held with other demonstrators and advisors to find some way of accelerating their effort. They decided the destruction of government property, particularly draft files, would be symbolic of their concerns. A lawyer in the group advised not to burn the files but to dump molasses or ink on them. According to some observers Thomas Merton, the Trappist monk and poet, and Martin Luther

King Jr., were consulted about the group's blood-pouring intentions and had approved.

"We thought using blood would be a very obvious thing for people to understand," said Philip. "We thought about the life-giving properties of blood and the fact that it is the symbol of life. Paradoxically the shedding of Christ's blood was a means to life. By pouring blood over those records, which are used to channel men into Vietnam and into murder or being murdered, we were affirming life and negating death."

"Did people understand the symbolism?" I asked.

"I think," answered Philip, "it was largely missed. It was called flamboyant, bizarre, and yet it grabbed some. It did bring people together in a mutual concern; a conspiracy of conscience I would say, and Catonsville grew out of that."

Philip was convicted of mutilating and destroying government records and interfering with the Selective Service programme. He was released on his own recognizance and sentencing was finally scheduled for May 27th, 1969. Then came Catonsville.

"I really didn't decide to join until about three days before," said Dan. "The decisions were all made by Phil and our Baltimore friends. I was sort of a late bloomer. They visited me and we talked things over. We sat up many hours at night talking. I had attended Phil's trial. I had been to Hanoi. I had seen a great deal. A friend of mine immolated himself. I didn't go through a lot of decision making, everything just sort of clicked into place very easily because of prior events. I had felt strangely on edge, waiting for something, and this was it."

On May 16th, just a few hours before the Catonsville raid, Daniel sent the manuscript for his new book *Night Flight To Hanoi* to the publishers. The subject of the book was his recent trip to North Vietnam, where he acted as intermediary in the release of two American prisoners of war. In the book's foreword, which he circulated to a few intimates, he anticipated and described the purpose of the raid. "Our apologies, good friends, for the fracture of good order, the burning of paper instead of children, the angering of the orderlies in the front parlor of the charnel house. We could not, so help us God, do otherwise. For we are sick at heart; our hearts give us no rest for thinking of the Land of Burning Children. And for thinking of that other Child, of whom the poet Luke speaks."

On May 17th Philip, Daniel and seven friends, known thereafter as the Catonsville Nine, entered the draft board of that small Baltimore area town. Ironically, the draft board rented space in the local Knights of Columbus building. When the nine arrived three women were at work on the records. They started to yell and began calling for the police through the window as the raiders loaded the draft records into wire baskets and carried them outside. In the parking lot the papers were soaked down with napalm and put to the torch. The napalm was concocted out of a mixture of soap flakes and gasoline as set out in an army handbook. When the police arrived the nine were standing around their bonfire reciting the Lord's prayer.

"Why did you not use blood again?" I asked.

"It had been misunderstood before," ansered Daniel. "Besides I think the decision to use napalm was a stroke of genius. All over the country this was the symbol of the horror of war. The eye of the hurricane of protest was around this napalm. It was the symbol of innocent death and the most horrendous form of death."

After their arrest Philip spent most of the summer in the federal penitentiary at Lewisburg, Pennsylvania thus becoming the first Catholic priest in American history to be jailed as a political prisoner. Pending trial, Daniel returned to his office at Cornell University.

"So much momentum had gathered by the time of our trial that it was an incredibly different scene from Phil's first one," said Dan. "There were a couple of thousand people in the streets all week in Baltimore. We had five excellent lawyers because they were anxious to get into a case like this. It was seen as a very important moment in history. We had tremendous support at Cornell, hundreds of students leaving classes all week and coming to Baltimore, then a powerful trial. We tried to remove all the ambiguity from it. We didn't waste time in denying anything. We wanted to make this a political forum. I think by and large it went very well. There was a lot of important writing done about the trial. Four or five books are being written about it. Cases of this sort are beginning to multiply which casts a good light backward upon the meaning of Catonsville as being a tremendous initiative in the war of resistance."

At the trial Daniel told the court that he had turned to civil disobedience as a last resort.

"I had been able to see by four years of very intense activity here that our government was able to surround, and to co-opt, and to suffocate any means of redress against the war that was legal."

He told the court that as a Christian at Cornell he could not be true to his ministry if he did not share the anguish of his students. "I saw suddenly that my position was false, that I was threatened with verbalizing my moral substance out of existence, that I too, was placing upon young soldiers the filthy burden of the original sin of war, that I too was asking them to become meat in a ceremony of death, so quite simply, I went to Catonsville, and this is why I am here."

The eloquent dialogue between the defendants and the judge at the trial won sympathy from the jury and audience alike, but it did not win acquittal. The jury was out only two hours and returned a "guilty as charged" verdict. Philip was sentenced to three and one-half years to run concurrently with the six he already had to serve. Daniel was sentenced to three years. An appeal was immediately launched.

On this crisp fall day in Syracuse the brothers were technically free. The mood was happy as suited the day. The feelings of thankfulness were genuine, but there was a cloud, an uneasiness that no one could ignore. Through the large front window of the brother's home we watched a dark car pull up and park on the opposite side of the street. "There he is again," said Phil. "The FBI keeps us in sight no matter where we go. They're afraid we'll take off and skip bail."

"What would really be the point of them putting you two in jail now anyway?" I asked. "It would just make martyrs out of you."

Daniel answered. "Well, I don't pretend to be able to get inside the purported minds of these people. One can never tell what they are thinking from day to day. Their response to people like us varies. One would think that something must occur within the heads of Mitchell or Nixon himself when he looks out from that bombshelter he lives in and sees half a million people passing his window saying "no" to the war, interrupting the football game he's trying to watch. Something must occur even within that head when he sees the draft board attacks increasing over the months. They are no longer just symbolic actions."

Philip interrupted. "You see, they're stuck with us. Our legal processes have by and large run out. If the Supreme Court refuses to review our case and the two appeals before them, then there will be no other recourse but to put us in jail. By that time the mileage we got out of the trial will have diminished somewhat and they will feel things have cooled down so we can be put away safely."

Daniel didn't let anything cool off. He continued lecturing, giving interviews and writing throughout the winter months. Appeals were denied and in March 1970, the group met to talk things over. The court had set April 9th as the day they would begin serving their sentences. On April 7th Dan went underground.

I was surprised to hear the news. Only a few months before he had told me how valuable jail could be to any movement. "We talk in America of 'sitting behind bars'. One does not literally sit there. There is a tremendous opportunity for political action from prison, also development, spiritual renewal. People have brought real change in the world from their prison cells from Ghandi to Bonhoeffer."

What had changed his mind? I suspect there were two reasons. Daniel felt he could keep the pot boiling more easily from the outside. He saw greater significance in a "resistance priest." He was simply better press on the run. He had also learned more about prison life. Philip was not placed in the low security work camp as had been expected but in Lewisburg's maximum security cells. Here he languished, cut off from fellow protestors and friends. He became frightened and depressed. Prison didn't hold the attraction for Daniel it once had.

I also recalled how during our interview both Daniel and Philip seemed to be questioning the continued use of court confrontation as a means of getting their message across.

"The trend now," said Philip, "seems to be for groups to disrupt a series of draft complexes, do very serious damage there, escape, go underground and then surface later on publicly. This is in the best tradition of civil disobedience and non-violence. They then declare themselves responsible in some public setting where they can do something with the press. In other words they can control the media and the message they hope to get out."

Daniel agreed. "You see tactics have changed so much in the short time since Catonsville. I feel the usefulness of the courtroom as a forum is pretty well exhausted. If we were just an example that keeps repeating itself, the government could then keep on prosecuting and grinding people under. But now we have something different. We have people who admit they did things without giving any details or without involving one another. The government simply doesn't have enough to go on, yet it's stuck with these admissions in public. So it's another very delightful non-violent tactic."

Philip added, "We are in a race between violence and non-violence in this country. When you have a society such as ours that generates a lot of violence, then logically the reaction is violent. The whole sabotage factor which is growing, such as all the bombings, is an indication of this. Young people are taking to the streets and forming angry mobs out of frustration with society and they are engaged in violent acts because it's the only thing they see that works. We are trying to counter that by using non-violent tactics such as disruption and public witness.''

Daniel's letters indicated he was enjoying the game of hide and seek with the FBI. He felt he had a definite role in "demythologizing Big Brother justice" and he liked the idea. He challenged J. Edgar Hoover to bring on the " 'copters, bugs, tapes and computers.'' He said he would claim a win even if captured and that he would go off to jail in better spirits than the arresting officers.

His family in Syracuse was under constant surveillance on the chance he might show up there. When his eighty-five year old mother was taken to hospital following an accident, day and night watches were posted by agents.

One hundred agents descended on the June wedding of two of Berrigan's friends and left empty handed after searching the church, including all the closets and the basement.

Daniel did a long interview for the *New York Times* and a half-hour interview for NBC. He met with groups of ministers and priests, students, professors, and of course resistors. Still the FBI couldn't find him. He continued writing letters, essays, articles and poetry which were eagerly published as "news from the underground.''

On one memorable occasion he surprised the congregation of First United Methodist Church in suburban Philadelphia by standing up one Sunday and delivering their sermon. He then vanished as mysteriously as he had appeared.

The embarrassed and frustrated FBI agents infiltrated the opening of the new play "The Trial of the Catonsville Nine" at the Los Angeles Music Centre Theatre. They felt this was the kind of event the elusive Daniel would find hard to miss. They were greeted by Daniel's voice taped earlier, welcoming everyone to the play and announcing cheerfully "your priest is in good spirits on a beautiful day.''

For four months he enjoyed playing his "scarlet pimpernel" role. He was sheltered by thirty-seven different families in ten cities, thereby implicating them and making them subject to prosecution for harbouring a convicted criminal.

His supporters were enchanted with this "spy who wouldn't come in from the cold.'' Enthusiastic journalists described him as Puck the mercurial, a modern Harry Houdini and a Count of Monte Cristo.

Finally FBI agents disguised as ornitholigists netted their bird in his sanctuary on Block Island at the home of friends Anthony Towne and lay theologian William Stringfellow.

With the Berrigan brothers both in Danbury Connecticut Federal Prison, the authorities relaxed in the belief their problems with these troublesome priests were over. This was not to be.

In January 1971 the Berrigan brothers were back in the headlines accused by the FBI of plotting to blow up the heating systems at five government sites in Washington, and to kidnap Henry Kissinger, who at that time was President Nixon's National Security Advisor, and hold him hostage until Nixon agreed to end the Vietnam War.

Friends and supporters of the Berrigans were indignant at the charges. While the brothers were certainly law breakers, it seemed inconceivable they would go against their professed non-violent approach to political protest. The brothers themselves denied their implication. Dan said, "There is absolutely nothing to it." Phil was more blunt and said it was "all bullshit."

In May, the United States Justice Department produced letters allegedly written by Philip, from the federal prison at Lewisburg, Pennsylvania where he was assigned before his transfer to Dansbury, to Sister Elizabeth McAlister, an art history teacher at Marymount College in Tarrytown, New York. The letters were illegally smuggled out by a trusted prisoner Boyd F. Douglas, who was permitted by officials to study during the day at nearby Bucknell University. Douglas co-operated with authorities and passed copies of the letters on to them after being promised immunity from prosecution.

The government said that at least ten letters were exchanged between Philip and Elizabeth between May and August 1970 in which plans to "make a citizen's arrest" of Henry Kissinger were outlined, in order to force a halt to B-52 bombing raids on Indo-China and to effect the release of political prisoners held in American jails. The possibility of filming a mock political trial of Kissinger then releasing the film to television stations was also mentioned in the letters. It was hard to believe that these intelligent and dedicated priests and their followers would deliberately plot such a bizarre scheme. Surely the government was bringing these charges to discredit the two priests who caused increased embarrassment to the administration as their time in prison developed into a full fledged martyrdom.

When the trial finally opened in January 1972, charges against Daniel were dropped and the prosecution concentrated on Philip, Sister Elizabeth and five others: Fathers Neil McLaughlin and Joseph Wenderoth, both Baltimore priests, Anthony Scoblick, a former priest, his wife Mary Cain Scoblick, a former nun, and Egbal Ahmad, a political science scholar from West Pakistan. The media promptly dubbed it the trial of the Harrisburg Seven.

At the trial Boyd Douglas testified he had met Berrigan when the priest entered Lewisburg Penitentiary in May of 1970. He explained how he had organized a mail drop and phone network to smuggle messages in and out for Berrigan and, when he became an FBI informant in June, he began opening and copying Berrigan's letters before passing them on. He also claimed that Philip had detailed plans on how to blow up some Washington underground utility tunnels.

The trial dragged on for eleven weeks. It became evident the prosecution didn't have or couldn't prove the evidence it touted so highly at the beginning. The entire event was becoming an embarrassment to the government. On the 1st of April Daniel Ellsberg, who had discovered secret Pentagon papers on American war policy, radical lawyer William Kunstler and Bella Abzug, U.S. Representative from New York, led a group of eight thousand anti-war protestors in a march on Washington to show support for the Harrisburg Seven.

When the verdict came in, Philip and Sister Elizabeth were the only defendants convicted. They were found guilty of smuggling a letter out of a federal prison "without the knowledge and consent of the warden on May 24, 1970." The jury remained deadlocked on all the other charges, but reporters learned later that they voted ten to two for acquittal.

An appeal was launched on two principal grounds: that the government's prosecution was discriminatory and that the government's case was "tainted" by their use of illegal wiretapping.

In August, U.S. District Judge R. Dixon Herman denied the motions for acquittal by writing, "in essence the defendants contend that the Department of Justice has maliciously sought prosecution of these defendants not for their criminal conduct alone, but because of their dedication to civil disobedience as a means of bringing the war to an end. They further classify their prosecution as an attempt to vindicate the former director of the Federal Bureau of Investigation." The judge said the defendants failed to prove either allegation. Sentencing was carried out the first week in September with Philip receiving two years and Sister

Elizabeth one.

At this point Philip had already served three years of his previous sentence and was eligible for parole. Since his new term was to run concurrently it would not interfere with his parole application.

One thing was certain. Locking up the Berrigans and their supporters seemed to cause as many problems for the administration as letting them go. By the end of the year they were all out on parole.

These years had unfolded like a movie script, and in the best tradition of Hollywood had a happy, romantic ending.

In May of the following year the *Baltimore Sun* reported that the Reverend Philip Berrigan and Sister Elizabeth McAlister were married in the New York apartment of the groom's brother the Reverend Daniel J. Berrigan. The Vietnam War and the Berrigans faded from the headlines at the same time. Was their fight over, the cause won, the lesson learned?

Daniel Berrigan today maintains the American government learned nothing from Vietnam. He says they have just changed their tactics and still intervene in other countries' internal affairs.

"The direction of the government after Vietnam is away from this crude landing of marines and gunboats and it's in the direction of internal subversion. That continues, so does economic control. It is in no sense a new act. It is a polishing up of the old act of aggression under other more acceptable, subtle and better concealed forms.

"The game has not changed, and I think we must always ground these kinds of observations in the use and misuse of our country and talents for our own people and others in the world.

"When we see the astonishing, brazen, continuing increase in the military budget and the neglect and rot afflicting our own people we have a very solid reason for believing nothing has changed.

"Vietnam only taught our government more skillful ways of presenting the same old United States force to the world.

"I am haunted these days by the feeling that there was a ghost hiding in the wings, ordering the Vietnam War and that ghost was 'the nuclear future, or non-future', of humanity. That ghost has now walked on stage in a most horrendous and inflated way to the point where now it seems to me the question of whether or not children are going to reach maturity is a grave one.

"This says to me that we have learned nothing from Vietnam. If we had, serious re-armament would not be on its way and both symbolic and real steps would be taking place instead of the run-away research, development, sales and stockpiling of nuclear arms that is terrifying the world.''

There is a strong feeling of dissillusionment in Dan Berrigan's tone as he speaks today. The causes he and his brother championed in the turbulent 1960's and 1970's seem to have faded as history has moved on to new crises and different calamities. But I think the Berrigans stood for more than mere protest against an unjust war. They were, and shall always be, models for people of Christian conscience who can no longer tolerate bureaucratic injustice, who take actions based on their convictions and who suffer for their faith.

What were the Berrigans all about? I think it was evident long ago, when Philip first found himself in court convicted of destroying government property, in November 1968.

In a passionate statement to the judge and jury just prior to sentencing, Philip Berrigan lashed out at his government and his church. ''We have but one message for our leaders in whose manicured hands the power of this land lies. Lead us. Lead us by giving people justice and there will be no need to break the law, no need for civil disobedience. Let President Nixon do what his predecessor failed to do; let him obey the rich less and the people more; let him think less of the privileged and more of the poor, less of America and more of the world. Let our bishops and religious superiors think less of buildings and more of people, less of causistry and more of the beatitudes, less of comfort and more of poverty, less of authority and more of service. Let lawmakers, judges and lawyers think less of law and more of justice, less of legal rituals and more of human rights.''

Claude Ryan

THE POPE
OF ST. SACREMENT
STREET

*I promised myself I would never become bourgeois
or a man too cut off from the ordinary people.*

I have never been able to figure out why so many people insist
that religion and politics don't mix. They are two of the most
interesting subjects basic to man and have, throughout history,
been interrelated. Yet we still hear of dinner party hosts banning
these two topics from conversation, and political candidates
worrying about Catholic, Protestant or Jewish reaction to election promises. Most politicians are eager to proclaim a "faith"
in their election literature and wear their church membership
badges proudly, at least until the votes are counted. Men of the
cloth have served Canada well as elected representatives, men
such as Tommy Douglas, a Baptist minister, Stanley Knowles
and David MacDonald, both United Church ministers and Roland
de Corneille, an Anglican priest.

Roman Catholic priests are being told by the Vatican not to
run for political office and to resign from those they hold. I re-

spect a priest's decision to resign and remain in the church, but find the ruling unfortunate.

Many of the priests and clergy throughout North America who hold public office bring a high level of concern for humanity and caring for the individual to the political arena. Most vote consistently for improved social conditions and for aid to the less fortunate throughout the world. If these men and women are removed from the political scene the gap may not be filled by people with that same humanitarian fervour.

The evangelical clergy tend to lean to the right, taking strong political stands against Communism, the Strategic Arms Limitation treaties and pushing for higher defense budgets and tighter immigration laws. They do not often run for office but prefer using pressure tactics such as Washington lobbies and providing financial and editorial support for conservative candidates. Television evangelists leave no doubt where their political sympathies lie, openly backing candidates who claim the born again experience and who promise an end to permissive legislation.

I asked Tommy Douglas if he knew why the claim was made that religion and politics don't mix. He answered, "One might think it had something to do with a desire for the separation of church and state, but more likely it's because they are two very volatile topics of conversation and can start an argument so much faster than a remark about the weather or vacation plans. They should mix, and indeed had better mix. If they don't, we are in deep trouble at the government level in this country."

One man, in whom religion and politics not only mix, but have become inseparable, is Claude Ryan, leader of Quebec's Liberal Party.

My interview with him in the spring of 1978 was meant only to present a portrait of this former newspaper editor who, after so many years as the conscience of Quebec, decided to stand for leader of a political party not renowned for its high degree of morality.

I liked him immediately when we met at the CBC studio in Montreal. His lean, craggy features, hooked nose and ready grin gave him the appearance of a friendly buzzard. He needed all the warmth he could muster on this occasion. There was a definite chill in the studio and it wasn't from the air conditioning. Members of the crew dutifully went about their work pointedly ignoring Ryan's outstretched hand. He was being shunned by Parti Québecois supporters. This was obviously not a new experience for him and his ebullient mood persisted.

Two things happened after the interview. First, crew members, who had turned their backs on him earlier, shook his hand politely with grudging admiration, impressed by his remarks during the taping.

The next reaction wasn't until a few months later when the interview went on the air as the opening programme of the *Man Alive* fall schedule.

Newspapers had a field day. "Claude Ryan talks to God! Did God tell Ryan to lead the Liberal Party? Does Claude Ryan hear voices?" the headlines read. In a six column spread, *Le Jour* proclaimed "C'est guidé par 'la main de Dieu' que Ryan a posé sa candidature à la direction du PL."

A cartoon in *Le Devoir* showed Ryan climbing a ladder through the clouds on his way to heaven answering "*L'appel.*" Another cartoon sketched the creation scene from the ceiling of the Sistine Chapel showing a nude Ryan touching fingers with God. It read, "La candidature de Ryan vue par Ryan — et Michel-Ange."

Columnist Thomas Schnumacher said Ryan was "more candid in this interview than he ever has been before," and added, "this is a personal talk that is all too rare with political figures."

I feel I should clear up any misunderstanding as to what was actually said by Claude Ryan and myself on that telecast.

I asked him how he made the decision to enter political life. He answered without hesitation.

"I think each man has to answer a few calls in his life. They come in more or less clear forms. Some human beings are privileged to see the call very, very clearly. Others do not have that privilege or redoubtable challenge. In my case it came very clearly and if I was to be a man of courage, I had to answer the call. But once you've done that you are as you were before. You're not better. You're not more courageous than other people. You have a kind of calm that suits your preparation and your usefulness in this particular stage in your development in the society in which you live."

Did he feel any kind of divine intervention?

"Oh yes. Oh yes," he answered. "I think that there is a divine guidance behind all that. For instance, if I am where I am today I think honestly it is because I answered other calls before. And I've always had a very, very profound faith in the unseen hand in these things. I don't think that God is carrying me by the hand all the time, no, but I think his word is manifested in several imperceptible manners which become clearer and clearer if you only have in yourself the quietness, the calm, that is required to discern that voice. There is a very mysterious interplay between the inner voice that is that of God within yourself and the things which you hear from your contemporaries. Very often the voice of God reaches you, not through those interminable soliloquies that you may have with yourself, but through listening to your neighbour, to your friends, to your relations, because they can be very good interpreters of what God wants you to do.''

"You have a sense of hearing that voice?'' I asked.

"Yes. If you recollect yourself, if you find those moments of silence and reflection, if you remain in touch with serious sources. It is very important that you go back to fundamental sources regularly, if you listen to your neighbours. I think a combination of all those sources will help you discern a certain will that is destined only for you, not for your neighbour, not for this or that, but you personally. I think that the great mystery of Christian experience in particular, and perhaps experience at large, is that you've got to make those decisions yourself. You can make them only for yourself. You're in conversation with a force which is way beyond your own world.''

I suppose his words are open to other interpretations, but there is no doubt in my mind that Claude Ryan feels he was directed by God to enter politics just as he had been directed in other areas of his life. He certainly seeks, and feels he receives, divine guidance.

Although this portion of the interview caused the greatest sensation in the press and in political circles, other parts of our conversation were equally revealing of Claude Ryan's nature.

I was interested in his personal story. What had his childhood been like? What about his marriage? He told me that his mother and father separated during the 1930's. These were depression years and the family was forced to go on welfare. His mother had to decide whether to send Claude and his two brothers out to work or get a job herself to pay for their education and the maintenance of a home. She chose the latter.

"My mother worked for twelve years until my brothers and I got a college education and were able to get along on our own. It was a great sacrifice. It influenced me to the extent that I decided to take my degree in social work and industrial relations because I was interested in social justice. I promised myself I would never become bourgeois or a man too cut off from the ordinary people.''

"Didn't you enter a monastery for a short time?'' I asked.

"Well, after I had graduated from college I announced that I would like to become a Benedictine monk, so, I went to a monastery about a hundred miles from Montreal. I spent one week there."

"Only a week?"

"Just a week. I could not sleep during those days. I could not digest the food. The life was much too secluded for me. You see, I thought that in a monastery I would have lots of time for study, but I discovered that I never had more than an hour for study at one time. The bell would ring and you had to go to the chapel for prayer, then another bell would ring and you had to go to the fields to work. So I thought to myself this is not the kind of life in which I'm interested. If you're reading a book that's three hundred pages long, you don't like to be interrupted every hour. So I rapidly concluded that this was not my calling at all. I think that it was a romantic dream I had conceived while a college student. I quickly forgot all about it."

"I heard that you didn't think you could handle the vow of obedience."

"Well, that was part of the thing too. I did not see myself obeying all those minute details of the Benedictine rule. It would have been too much for me to bow before the Abbot whenever I had to pass before him. It would not have been my style. I have great admiration for those who can do that in the name of God for very supernatural motives, but I realized it was not my calling."

The church did, however, remain a large part of Ryan's life. For seventeen years he worked for Catholic Action, a lay organization devoted to translating Roman Catholic philosophy into deeds through social service. It was during that time he decided to marry. Once the decision was made he wasted no time in selecting a wife.

"I discovered my wife in the Catholic Action organization. She was a leader in one of our movements, when I was general secretary. I had reflected for many years about whether I should get married. Finally at the age of thirty-three I decided I should. The time had come. We had several very fine women in the Catholic Action organization. They had the kind of social and intellectual training that would make remarkable wives and this person was in that milieu. I had heard a lot of nice things said about her by others in the organization so I invited her to dinner one Sunday and told her frankly that I wanted a wife and was choosing her."

"You mean you chose her right there and told her you wanted to marry her?"

"Yes. I told her right away and she wept. I wept too. Six months later we were married and we've never looked back, or elsewhere, since!"

Ryan of course became best known as editor and publisher of *Le Devoir* the very influential Montreal daily. For fourteen years Ryan was a force to be reckoned with in Quebec public affairs. His long, detailed editorials earned him the title "the conscience of Quebec." I mentioned that many in English Canada seemed to have built him into a saviour of Quebec.

"Practically all imaginable labels have been applied to me over the years. I was once denounced as a traitor by a member of parliament for Toronto. That was in the October crisis of 1970. He asked that I be brought before the courts on charges of treason. I don't like labels."

"Well, like it or not," I said, "you have been labelled the "conscience of Quebec," the "Pope of St. Sacrement Street." We all know you as a very religious man and now you've thrown your hat into the political ring. How are you going to handle this change of roles?"

"I think, if I had become involved in politics fifteen years ago it would have been more dangerous. At fifty-three I have become stable in my convictions, my character, my way of doing things. It is much more difficult to change a man at this age than if he were thirty-five and ambitious to get into power. I don't have any lust for power. I am not as blinded by the realities of power as I would have been twenty years ago. I've seen so many men come and pass in this area of politics that I am no longer naive about it."

"You seem to be really sold on the idea that a Christian should be involved in the world and certainly in politics. What about the saying that religion and politics don't mix?"

"I have learned over the years that the world in which you and I are evolving is only a world of appearance. The real world is much more profound and that is the world of God. In that world we are surrounded and penetrated by the reality of God in all we do. And once you've been penetrated by that reality, whether you're in politics, or trade unions, or in a competitive business, there is always this added dimension to your actions. It doesn't mean you are going to act in a perfect manner, but you have a base from which to operate and where you can return in order to reflect on your actions and to try and improve upon what you did the previous day."

"You do make mistakes and slide back from time to time?"

"Oh yes indeed. Several times a day, on my best days. The problem is finding time to reflect. When you are as deeply involved in things as I am, especially now in politics, but it was basically the same when I was in charge of *Le Devoir*, you feel the need to get back into yourself in complete solitude. I am the kind of person who can keep running for five or six days without any interruption but then on the sixth, or seventh or eighth day, depending on my schedule, I have to find time to reflect. Then, I will shut the door of my study at home, begin reading the Bible or writings by religious authors and I find one becomes born again more or less; that is born again to the things you cherish the most."

I had heard from a lawyer friend of Ryan's that he agonized over decision making. I asked him if this was true.

"Look," he said, "when principles are involved I have no difficulty reaching a decision very, very rapidly. The other day I read an important government document of about five hundred pages. Within an hour or two I had made up my mind what I should say about it, because fundamental principles were involved and they are very clear in my mind. When it comes to more personal decisions, which are going to have great consequences both for myself and my fellow man, then I have to think a great deal. I call these my fifty-one, forty-nine decisions. There are fifty-one chances that I might make the right decision and forty-nine that I might make the wrong one. So I have to agonize trying to see both sides in order to reach the best possible conclusion. Those who know me closely are appalled by that at times. They say where the hell is he going to land? On the final day that I have set for a conclusion I see the light, put it in writing and never look back."

I asked him if he prayed at all in making a decision.

"Yes I do," he answered, "but not in as prolonged a manner as I used to when I was in Catholic Action. There my life was organized in such a way that I had at least an hour each day to spend in religious exercise. Today I don't have that kind of time. I may spend five days without finding the time to pray. During this time there will be short interruptions when I'll think to myself, 'Oh God help me in this matter' or 'Thank you God for helping me with this or that,' but that's not real prayer in my view. To pray, you have to attain a certain tranquility of soul and that doesn't come about suddenly. You have to have time. My problem is I have to move from one conversation to another, one telephone call to another, one trip to another, and the periods which I would like to have for prayer and meditation are not long and not numerous enough. I'm living on stock which I accumulated over the years. I wish I had more time."

Time was precious to Claude Ryan at this particular moment in Quebec's history. When we did this programme he had not yet gained the solid footing he was to later. The referendum was still in the future. His every waking hour became a whirlwind of meetings, speeches, planning sessions and highly charged debates on the future of his beloved province. The quiet minutes for meditation and prayer were rare indeed.

In the turbulent world of politics it was refreshing to find a man of high principles with a deep conviction about the shape of the society he envisioned.

"I would like a society," he told me, "in which freedom remains the fundamental value. There are two great schools of thought in politics and both can appeal to a Christian person. One will lay emphasis on liberty and the other will emphasize equality. In the name of equality you may be tempted to curtail freedom in several areas, not because you are a barbarian or a dictator, but because you want to give everyone an equal chance. I prefer to put liberty first. I think that liberty, which derives from the human dignity of an individual, is much more fundamental. There must be room for certain differences among men, in terms of station in life, income, intellectual development, the kind of family commitments they might have, et cetera, and I think you have a better view of the extent to which you should extend equality if your convictions are solidly rooted in the concept of liberty."

Sondra Diamond

I AM NOT
WHAT YOU SEE

*Dear Sir, This is likely the first letter you
have ever received from a vegetable.*

At its best, the *Man Alive* programme touches people in a way
that encourages them to re-examine their attitudes and beliefs.
It challenges them to look at preconceived notions, helps them
understand their neighbour. It moves them toward more humane
behaviour. It pricks their consciences. It stirs their emotions.

One programme stands out above the others in meeting all
these objectives — my interview with Sondra Diamond.

That programme's accomplishments are significant. It drew
thousands of letters, the largest response in *Man Alive's* history.
It attained the largest number of foreign sales of any CBC programme at that time. It won more awards than any other *Man
Alive* show. It is still remembered and commented upon by viewers in every part of Canada, and it launched Sondra Diamond on
an extensive speaking tour to aid the handicapped.

It all started with a letter written by Sondra to the editor of
Newsweek. The magazine had published an article about mercy

killing which included statements from medical men suggesting that some babies, severely retarded at birth, should be allowed to die instead of living on as human vegetables. Sondra's letter began "Dear Sir, This is likely the first letter you have ever received from a vegetable." She then went on to tell her story.

We were, at that time, putting together a programme on the "meaning of humaness" and decided to ask Sondra to fly from Philadelphia to Toronto for an interview. As the programme was already near completion only a few minutes would be needed. Negotiations were concluded and a recording date set.

All we really wanted to do was introduce her to the viewers as an example of someone who, although labelled "less than human" and despite medical opinion and the hurdles of society, not only survived, but flourished.

It would be a brief recording session, just a few questions from me to help her along. We really didn't expect any more than a little personal experience story to fill a small hole in an existing programme.

The producer explained to me what I might expect. "She's thirty-seven years old," he said. "At birth she suffered severe mental and physical defects. Attending doctors urged her parents to let her die, since she would never be able to function normally. Her parents consulted doctors in Philadelphia, Baltimore and New York, until they finally found one who thought Sondra was worth saving. He diagnosed her condition as cerebral palsy and told her parents she would never be able to walk, feed herself, toilet herself or talk properly. But, she was educable."

"How will she sound on air? Will the viewers be able to understand her speech?"

"Yes, if she goes slowly. I talked with her on the phone. Her speech is slurred and halting, but understandable. She's a practicing psychologist you know; a very bright girl. She doesn't look very good though. The burns, I suppose, don't help."

"Burns!" Suddenly I was worried. "What burns?" My worry seemed contagious. My producer hurriedly explained, "When she was a sophomore in college she was filling a cigarette lighter with fluid when it caught fire. She's not very dexterous, but she tries to do things for herself. Some of the fluid had dripped on her clothes. Since she couldn't move, she just sat there screaming and burning until help came. She suffered burns to over fifty per cent of her body. They expected her to die. Her parents were advised to let her die rather than go through the extensive and costly skin grafts. However, Sondra and her parents persisted until the work was done. Why does this upset you so much?''

I had worked with many handicapped people and knew several personally. I was in no way repulsed or upset to be in their company. But grafted skin was another matter. Ever since I was a child, whenever I saw it, I simply passed out.

A one armed man working in a factory once showed me his stomach where skin had been removed to patch up his severed stump. I woke up a few minutes later sprawled on the cement factory floor.

Once, visiting a friend in the hospital, he showed me how the scarred tissue was closing 'nicely' over his incision. I almost made it to the door, but not quite. Doctors and nurses came running as I hit the deck. Another time, I was at a carnival in New York state which featured a side show of various attractions. One was a man who had supposedly been captured by a band of aborigines in Central America, who removed large portions of his skin for drum-heads. I took one look at his tissuepaper-like features and everything went black.

For some strange reason I cannot look at scarred tissue or grafted skin. I've learned to simply avoid looking at people in this condition.

''We may have a problem,'' said my producer.

Sondra and her mother arrived in Toronto and headed directly for the studio. The crew was briefed; warned that this interview might be difficult to shoot because of her spasmodic, uncontrollable movements. The studio doors opened and in came Sondra in a self-propelled wheel chair accompanied by her mother. She was dressed simply but attractively in a high neck dress with long sleeves. My grafted skin phobia would not be a problem. Not a scar in sight.

Even to this day people ask, ''What was your first impression of Sondra? How did you feel?''

I can honestly say that I felt no different than I do in any other interview situation. Here was a person with a story to tell. Hopefully, I could make her feel at ease and ask the kinds of questions that would elicit interesting responses. When the lights are on and cameras are rolling you just try to make a programme that viewers will watch and benefit from. Personal feelings have very little to do with it.

''Tell me about yourself Sondra,'' I said.

''I'd be happy to,'' she replied. And the interview was under-way.

''I have a Masters Degree in Psychology. I'm in private practice. I'm very happy with this work but it is a compromise. I made many attempts to get a job working with agencies or other professionals, but have been turned down every time. They're not subtle about it. They explain that, while I have the educational credentials, the expertise, they cannot hire me because of the cosmetics of my body. So, in order to fulfill myself professionally, I've had to set up in private practice.''

"You used the word 'vegetable' in your letter to *Newsweek*. I can imagine how you feel about that word. Was there a time in your life when you came to realize that society considered you less than human?''

"I remember a particular incident that happened when I was about nine. My mother was helping me off the school bus and there was a lady standing on the side walk watching this very complicated procedure. She was shaking and pointing at me and saying, 'Oh my God look! Oh my God!' My mother turned to her and snapped, 'we charge a quarter to see this!' ''

"When we got in the house I asked my mother what all that had been about and she said, 'Sondra, that lady is looking at what she thinks is a freak.' I asked her 'Is that the way you see me?' My mother answered, 'no. Your dad and I have never seen you that way. But that is how other people will see you.' ''

I think that warning from Sondra's mother has likely influenced her entire life. She seems to expect everyone to see her as a kind of curiosity. Some do, of course, and these experiences have also added to her defensiveness. She recounted an incident in a restaurant when a woman approached her and imitated her palsied movements. The woman shook her body and arms, then inquired, "Why are you doing that? Why are you in that wheel chair?" Sondra answered in mock surprise, "What do you mean? Wheel chair? What wheel chair? I don't see any wheel chair!" The woman just walked away confused and Sondra said she felt tremendous.

We talked at some length about humaness. How would she define it?

"Humaness in our society, as I see it, is to have a beautiful body, blue eyes, blonde hair and be structurally straight. It means you are expected to do certain self-help tasks, toilet yourself, feed yourself, things I cannot do, and I certainly don't have a beautiful body. It means living up to other people's expectations. Society also says that one of the requirements of humaness is success. My parents were advised not to waste money on my education since I wouldn't be able to do anything with the knowledge. That was not the point. I just wanted to have an education. As a psychologist I'm often called upon to give IQ tests. When these are given to disabled children there are no valid results. One of the questions for example asks 'What do you do if you find a stamped and addressed letter on the street.' A handicapped child of seven or eight has not been outside of his own home. He has no street experience and therefore cannot integrate this kind of information. On most IQ tests the child must be able to speak in order to answer the questions. We have many children who cannot. I have a recordable IQ on the verbal score of one hundred and forty. The other half of the test, the performance score, manipulating blocks and putting together pieces of puzzles, I have a zero. I cannot do it. So what are you measuring? There are those who say if you have an IQ of less than twenty you are not human. I know people personally, with whom I interact, whose IQ's cannot be measured, yet to be with them is an exciting and lovely experience.

"I am sure that we have not developed sophisticated enough instruments yet to measure humaness. We don't know what's going on inside a person. If a child enjoys the sensation of the bedsheets against his skin, as I do, or if he enjoys the sensation of someone touching him while changing his diapers, he is knowing life. Can we deny this knowledge of life to anyone?

"To come to an understanding of humaness, or to decide who is human, the only essential thing is to make no assumptions. Don't decide what they are until you interact with them. I don't know how you felt when you first saw me. I'm sure you had some initial gut reaction which I would like you to share with me if we have time. Some people tell me, 'Gee, when I first met you I thought you were an idiot!' To decide who or what is human then, is to make no assumptions, to have no expectations. Just do the best you can for them medically, educationally, psychologically and lovingly."

We talked a bit about her parents and how supportive and loving they were. Sondra's parents have been faced with much more than the normal trials of bringing up a daughter. It is obvious that they must possess great reserves of strength and energy to draw on in their lives. Their first decision to fight for their daughter's life seems like a code they have kept throughout. The psychological pain, the physical effort and the perpetual care involved have not made the Diamonds bitter. They are always there with encouragement for every new hurdle Sondra attempts.

Sondra had real fears about what would happen to her when

her parents were no longer around, whether or not she would be able to afford the constant help required.

The American government has built-in support systems for the handicapped, but they are rarely able to supply the quality of care that Sondra receives from her parents. It is fortunate that she had the drive and ability to become a professional psychologist. She will in all likelihood have the funds to hire the help she desires. Her fear, however, is understandable for without this help she could not survive.

I asked her about her moments of despair. There must be times when the helplessness and the frustrations of her life become unbearable.

"It happens about every six months. My family has come to expect it. I go into my room and lock the door and I sit for a couple of hours. I ask myself 'Why am I fighting so hard?' Inside of me I am not a disabled person. I am not what you see. I am a woman inside, a woman with professional drives, sexual drives, all kinds of drives. I get to the point where I can't stand people saying you cannot do this. Stop. This is as far as you can go. Then, I need to sit down by myself and cry for a while. Self pity is very therapeutic for me. Then I am able to say, 'Okay, let's go on from here, let's keep going'."

Throughout the interview I was very moved by Sondra's words and filled with admiration for her courage and determination. I also appreciated her frankness in answering all my questions.

By necessity a television studio is a quiet place during the taping of an interview, but there are times during particularly moving or intensely interesting encounters when the stillness becomes almost visible. This was one of them. The attention of every crew member was rivetted on this small, twisted, shaking figure. The air was charged with emotion and everyone hushed in awe.

I said, "You asked what my reaction was to you when you first came in. Well Sondra, I had an idea what you would look like, so that didn't bother me, but I had no idea what you would say or how we would interact. You said earlier in the interview that you certainly aren't beautiful. I'd like to contradict that. I think you are a most beautiful person. Thank you very much for coming on our programme."

"Thank you," said Sondra, and the interview was over. As soon as the cameras stopped Sondra asked, "How was I?"

"Just fine," I assured here, "You handled the questions extremely well."

"That's an advantage I have," she laughed. "I shake so much

82

all the time, that no one can tell when I'm nervous.''

Two years passed before I saw Sondra again. A great deal had happened in the interim. The programme which was titled appropriately ''I Am Not What You See'' had been repeated on *Man Alive* twice due to viewers' requests. CTV and other private stations carried excerpts from it. Public Broadcasting in the United States, European and Australian networks had also broadcast it. An enterprising American illegally recorded the show and was caught pedalling it for $300 a copy to people and organizations involved in work with the handicapped. His downfall came when he inadvertently offered to sell Sondra a tape and she immediately contacted us.

By this time Sondra had made the rounds of the American talk shows and was in great demand as a speaker at conferences and seminars all over North America. One of these appearances was at a conference of nurses, doctors and teachers in Toronto in the spring of 1976, organized by the Hospital for Sick Children. The hospital asked if I would arrange for the audience to screen ''I Am Not What You See'' and also moderate a panel discussion on the handicapped in our society. I, of course, agreed.

We contacted Sondra before the event to ask about the possibility of arranging another interview. To our surprise she made a strange request. ''Would it be possible,'' she asked, ''to have someone other than Bonisteel do the interview?''

''But, why?'' asked the producer. ''I thought you and Roy got along so well.''

''Because I think it would be better to use a regular interviewer instead of a professional actor this time,'' she replied.

He explained that I was the regular host and interviewer for the *Man Alive* series and was not an actor brought in for the occasion. What made her think I was?

''I just didn't think anyone could show that much compassion and accept me so warmly unless he was putting on an act,'' she said.

My producer assured her that everyone associated with the programme, including millions of viewers, had reacted in the same way. No one was acting. We sincerely liked her.

With these assurances she agreed to meet me on camera again. I was surprised at Sondra's conviction that I had been acting. I could only attribute it to our programme being her first television experience and her subsequent appearances on American programmes presumably had not produced the same effect on her interviewers. To sit across from Sondra while she reveals her innermost feelings with such passion and insight and not be moved seems to me impossible.

The conference was well attended, and Sondra received a standing ovation when her wheel chair was pushed up a special ramp to the microphone.

With a keen sense of humour she recounted stories of her childhood and relations with her parents.

She told the audience, "I have never felt it was intrinsically a burden to be disabled. It only seemed to me that society in its lack of accommodation made it a burden. I recall as a child not feeling particularly different from other children. I was aware that I couldn't do the same things they could, but I didn't feel especially bad about it. This was likely due to the fact that I had very supportive parents. No matter what struggles or fights I had in the outside world, I could always come home and be reassured by my parents that the fight was worth it. Open communication between the parent and the disabled child makes it so much easier for both of them.

"I remember the first time I ever travelled alone. I was sixteen years old and some friends in Baltimore invited me to come and visit them. I sat down with my parents and asked how they felt about this. It was a difficult decision for them. I understood that, but I had to try my wings. They understood. I'll never forget the day I left. My father settled me into the train seat, then stood on the platform waving good-bye. He was trying not to cry and to be very brave about the whole thing and so was I. The train started to pull out of the station and after we had gone two or three blocks, I looked back, and there was my father waving with one hand and leaning on my wheel chair with the other. He had forgotten to put it on the train. I yelled, 'Stop this train!' A conductor, who was passing through the car and had seen me being carried aboard, understood the situation and pulled the emergency cord. I asked, 'Could you back up the train please, and get my wheel chair?' He did. We got back to the platform and there was my father still standing there waving good-bye and leaning on my wheelchair. It wasn't until the conductor went over to him and said 'Excuse me, may we have the wheel chair?' that my father suddenly realized what had happened.

"I don't know how many gray hairs my parents have acquired as the result of raising a disabled child, but I think they would say it has been worth it, for they have seen me grow and develop and this has given them pleasure.

"It is true that I need a lot of physical help, but I have been armed by my parents with a strong sense of self-confidence and more important, an awareness that it's alright to need help and to ask for it.''

Following her opening remarks I began the panel discussion with Dr. Paul Steinhouer, Senior Staff Psychiatrist from the hospital, Mrs. Isabel Otter, the mother of a handicapped child, and Sondra.

Sondra challenged the audience to examine their own personal feelings toward the disabled. How did they feel about the facial grimaces or saliva on their clothing? How did they feel being salivated on?

"As hard as you may try," she said, "you will not be able to hide your feelings from the disabled individual with whom you are working. He will perceive your feelings in the way you touch him and the way you relate to him verbally. A disabled person knows how someone feels about him from the way he is lifted, or helped on with his clothing.''

I asked Dr. Steinhouer why people reacted the way they did toward the disabled, why some people according to Sondra showed signs of repugnance.

"I think there are two basic components to our reactions," he answered. "First, many of us have a basic fear of a malformation, handicap, injury or deformity happening to us. Most of the time we repress this and just don't think about it. When we see someone who has an obvious malformation or handicap of some sort it stirs up our anxiety and causes discomfort. At some level there is an identification with that person and we think 'that could be me,' and we deal with our own anxiety with a mixture of fascination and repulsion.

"At the same time, we are also faced with a social encounter different than what we are used to and we don't really know the rules. We are dealing with a fascination, a compelling interest that makes it hard to keep our eyes off a person who is looking different or behaving in a way that is strange to us. On the other hand, we've been taught that it is not polite to stare and if we're sensitive people, as many of us are, there is a fear of embarrassing or hurting the other person. We don't know the cues for this strange sort of social situation. We don't know what is expected of us and we become socially disoriented.''

Isobel Otter agreed, and added, "The parents have a very odd position to play as spectator to the handicapped person and the public reaction. As a parent he feels very protective and responsible for his disabled child. His problem is how to deal with this appropriately to help the child cope in this situation and at the same time educate the public so they will gradually accept the handicapped as persons.''

This prompted Sondra to comment on the stereotype people held concerning the handicapped in regard to their sexuality.

''To me the most important thing is that you relate to me as a total human being. I am a woman. Most people see me as asexual, or neuter, neither male or female. I happen to be female, and I'm also heterosexual. I would like to be related to on a heterosexual level. I don't feel this from most people. When I have encounters with men any sensual feelings I have are obviously picked up by them. I am not a poker face. But the reaction from them is usually the same, 'Sondra you are a wonderful person, you should become a nun.' They don't know how to cope with any sexual feelings they might have or I might have toward them, so they would like to put me off in a convent some place where they wouldn't have to deal with them.''

Isobel Otter pointed out that it wasn't just the general public who saw the physically disabled as neuter, parents did as well.

''Parents are so overwhelmed with the physical and medical problems of their child that they quite often completely forget the sexual aspect of his life. It is quite a shock for some parents to learn that their child has sexual needs. Parents and counsellors should start dealing with this problem at a very early age.''

Sondra agreed and related an incident that occurred to her when she was thirteen.

''At that time I was still getting physical therapy in this special school and I was assigned to a male physical therapist. I found it very sexually stimulating. He was a young and handsome man. I found I couldn't concentrate on the exercises so I went to the chief therapist, who was a woman, and asked if I could have a female therapist. She asked why, 'Don't you like Mr. Smith?' I said, 'Oh, yeah, I like him a lot, that's the problem.' I couldn't make her understand that I had these very upsetting feelings and she would not change my therapist.''

Sondra paused, looked out over the attentive audience and with a mischievous twinkle in her eye continued, ''and now Mr. Smith and I are married with three children and live happily in Manhattan.'' There was a short silence and then a burst of enthusiastic applause as the people understood the joke.

Over the wave of laughter Sondra said, ''People just can't imagine the disabled having these sexual feelings. We are indeed looked upon as neuter.''

At the close of the conference I had an opportunity to chat at some length with Sondra and be brought up to date on her activities. She was devoting a great deal of her time to working with associations for the handicapped. She had become a living example of hope to many.

"For me it is primarily a selfish thing," she insisted. "I want to exist. I want to eat in restaurants. I want to make a living, so I go around saying 'hey, you can't discriminate against the disabled. Hey, you should employ the disabled.' I'm doing this for myself too. I want to create an environment where I can live. By easing the struggle of others, I ease my own struggle."

The Karen Ann Quinlan case was very much in the news at this time, and Sondra had publicly expressed her views on the issue.

In 1975 twenty-one year old Karen Ann lapsed into a comatose condition for reasons still unknown today. Her parents are not sure whether it was caused by the combination of tranquilizers and alcohol, a sugar condition, exposure to lead at work, or a hard fall on concrete steps. After assurances a year later that she would not recover and would likely suffer from severe brain damage if she did, her parents requested she be taken off the hospital respirator machine and be allowed to live, or die on her own without "extraordinary measures." Doctors refused so the Quinlans filed a petition in the United States Supreme Court to force the action.

Experts testified at the trial that Karen Ann was not dead because brain activity had not ceased but that she would surely die if the respirator was removed and this would constitute murder. The Supreme Court in a landmark decision ruled that the respirator could be removed if a medical ethics committee determined there was no reasonable possibility of Karen's recovery. It was removed in May 1976 and today Karen continues to live, though is still unable to respond.

Her body has shrunk to sixty-eight pounds and her eyes, sometimes open, sometimes closed, stare unseeingly, but she is not being kept alive by machines.

Mr. and Mrs. Quinlan say their daughter symbolizes the care terminally ill patients should have and that by asking for removal of the respirator they showed a respect for life and, if it happens, death with dignity.

Sondra had spoken out very decisively against the right of anyone to remove life-sustaining equipment. I asked her why she took this stand.

"The case interests me because it parallels the cause of and for the physically disabled. As disabled people we are victimized in terms of the 'pulling of the plug' syndrome. The attitude is 'Well, they're going to be disabled anyway, why use extraordinary means to keep them alive?' So we are prime targets for 'death with dignity.' I'm probably not looking at the case objectively because I'm looking at it from my point of view.

"As I see it, when we talk about death, using terms such as 'dignity' and 'humanhood' we are making it sound like a marvelous thing. The next step is to decide who will die and who will live. We allow the disabled to die and the infirm and those who will be a burden on society. If that's where our heads are at, what does it say about our fellow man? What we are saying is, 'As soon as you stumble and fall we're going to throw you down the toilet. So you had better be straight and strong and healthy and good or you are of no use anymore.' "

I wondered if Sondra still had those lonely times of depression she told me about in our first meeting. Did she still need to shut herself into her room as much as ever?

"The problem now is that I don't get much private space. We all need this. Able bodied people can walk around and nobody notices them. I am always being looked at. My private space is being invaded constantly, so I still need to retreat now and again and regroup. I don't mind the travelling and the speaking and the writing. It's the exposing yourself to others that is hard. I don't like being on display, showing myself to people all the time. There are private parts to me that I want to keep unexposed, but, when you are committed to a cause you can't stay hidden very long. You've got to get out there and be exposed."

We said goodbye with a promise to keep in touch. I chatted with her on the phone in the spring of 1980. She was in good spirits and working hard.

"About twenty-five percent of my time is devoted to attending conferences for the disabled and speaking at special seminars and workshops. I enjoy doing this, particularly when I come to Canada. I had a marvelous time in Edmonton, Alberta last fall."

"What about your practice?" I asked. "Are you still seeing patients?"

"Yes indeed. It is flourishing, growing larger all the time."

"Would you consider doing another *Man Alive* programme?"

"Certainly, I would enjoy very much working with you again."

I'm interested to find out what the future holds in store for Sondra Diamond and I suspect *Man Alive* viewers would also like to know.

One has to admire a person who has succeeded, against all odds, at proving herself human; not approximately human or "doesn't she do well for a cripple," but, simply human. She is not without the same drives, the same dimensions of character, the same attributes and, dare I say it, the same faults as any other human being. Was this not her goal? Did she not, in fact, dedicate her life to proving her humaness?

In her we see a tremendous strength, a contagious sense of humour and a real concern for others, as handicapped as she is. We also see a woman who is less than generous with strangers troubled by her appearance; who is not above instilling a sense of guilt in those she meets.

We give her no credit at all if we call her perfect, or a saint. She isn't. To label her so is to ignore Sondra Diamond in her totality.

Yes, she is someone to be admired. She represents the strength of the human will. But she does not have to be looked at with the same incredulity as a chimpanzee who has learnt to count by rote. She can be understood as can a prisoner of war who cannot overcome the trauma of a living hell. They have a problem. We can deal with this. Never do we deny them the right to be troubled. We never ignore the rest of their character which has left Auschwitz far behind. We must leave Sondra Diamond's personal Auschwitz behind and deal with her as a person; a complete person.

Gordon Sinclair & George Johnston

THE
SINCLAIR-JOHNSTON
DEBATE

As the cut and thrust of the discussion heated up, I became less a moderator and more of a spectator at a verbal tennis tournament.

Inevitably, when I am chatting with people anywhere in Canada, the question is asked "What is Gordon Sinclair really like?" My reply is always the same. "I don't know Gordon very well, so I can't answer that. But personally I like him very much."

Our paths have crossed several times and my respect and admiration for him has increased over the years. His career as a journalist, reporter and broadcaster is unmatched and his outspoken opinions are legendary.

We first met in a television studio to tape what was later to become one of the most popular and delightful episodes of *Man Alive*.

Reverend George Johnston, professor of New Testament at McGill University, expressed a desire to meet with Sinclair and challenge some of his quoted views on Christianity. Gordon accepted the proposal and the two squared off one afternoon shortly after New Years in 1968. As the cut and thrust of the discussion heated up, I became less a moderator and more of a spectator at a verbal tennis tournament.

Many people did not know that Gordon had been a church member for over twenty years. He even taught Sunday School at one time. This was in the Methodist denomination. He continued in the United Church for about four years after it was formed in 1925.

Johnston claimed that Gordon's views of religion were formed in this early Sunday School environment and were not relevant in today's less conservative church atmosphere. As a liberal theologian Johnston could not and would not defend a literal understanding of some biblical passages.

"What I'm against," said Gordon, "is the dogma of the Christian. I think dogma is a mistake. It's too all embracing. I think some parts of the Christian religion are degrading to its own members. For example, the Anglicans saying 'I am a miserable sinner.' They make this public admission as part of their creed. Well, I don't see why a person has to degrade himself in that way. To me it's not in the spirit of man."

Johnston: "What do you mean by dogma? That word has a specialized meaning. Which meaning do you give the word?

Sinclair: I mean there are certain things you are required to believe without access to your own judgment. Now, you can quote Greek and Latin and so on, I didn't go to high school, so you have a great advantage on me there. You have the advantage of education but my idea is that when the church says, 'this is it' you are required to believe it. Am I right?

Johnston: Only up to a point. A dogma is a fact or decision made by a council or some other kind of church authority after a process of discussion by people. The people, the presbytors, the deacons, the bishops, all have a long discussion about anything before it becomes a decision.

Sinclair: But isn't a Christian, for example, required to believe that his saviour Christ rose in the physical flesh from the dead after some days?

Johnston: No he is not. Some kinds of Christians are.

Sinclair: Then they're the only ones I have met. With them there is no 'maybe I believe.' It's 'you must believe it.'

Johnston: I'm not a fundamentalist. I am a liberal and catholic christian. I happen to be a minister of the United Church of Canada, but I do not believe in the physical resurrection.

Sinclair: Well, that's what I was taught and what millions of

91

people are being taught at this hour. Billy Graham thinks it's a great idea. What do you think of Graham?

Johnston: I don't want to express an opinion of a man who is not here to defend himself, but I would say he is an old-fashioned conservative Christian who has not taken the measure of biblical scholarship, and since he hasn't I would have to disagree with him greatly, just as I would disagree with you if you don't have up to date biblical and theological insight and knowledge."

Gordon kept pushing Dr. Johnston into explanations of Old Testament myths, demanding whether or not he believed in heaven, hell, original sin, the Garden of Eden, and the six day creation of the world. Johnston swatted these points away as if they were pesky mosquitoes and demanded a discussion "higher than the level of a Methodist Sunday School in 1905."

"All right then," said Gordon, "tell me, do you believe in prayer? Do you believe your prayers will be answered to help you in human affairs?"

Johnston: "I believe that God is in you, in you Gordon Sinclair. God's spirit is in you. You might not recognize it, but God is in everybody and in some mysterious way he is the influence and power in human life, a kind of driving force.

Sinclair: Well where was he then when six million Jews were slaughtered by Adolph Hitler?

Johnston: I'll tell you where he was. He was in the gas chamber with the first victim. God was in every one of the six million victims. God is involved in the suffering of the world. He is the first sufferer. He knows more about suffering than any of us can. That's the kind of God I believe in.

Sinclair: Six million Jews processed like hogs and you say God was there. They were all praying to God to save them, 'Mercy, have mercy on me. Protect me from this evil that is coming.' All processed, and you say God was there? And this is a kind God?

Johnston: God was there. You see Gordon, you are working with a concept of God that is partly devilish, partly compassionate and partly ignorant....

Sinclair: And partly from seeing millions of people starve to death. In India, for example, and in China. I was there.

Johnston: I've seen it in India too. I've been there. But let me say this. I don't believe in the kind of God who does intervene to save millions, or even one, at least in the way you would like him to. I think that creation is intended to be a real crea-

92

tion of the individual person, with individual responsibility and social responsibility. Chance operates to a large extent, scientists will tell you that. The chance factor is there. I think God has it there because there is no other way we could be people. Now, who is responsible for killing six million Jews? Not God, but the Nazis!

Sinclair: God could have prevented it.

Johnston: No he can't, because if he tried to prevent it, in that way, he takes away our responsibilities.

Sinclair: So he is a powerless God then.

Johnston: Nope, I think God is the most intelligent and the most involved being there is in the universe. And it's his intelligence which prevents him from interfering like a magician.

Sinclair: Well that's very convenient. He doesn't do anything. He just lets six million get killed.

Johnston: I didn't say he did nothing. Yes, he lets the six million get killed. I agree with you there. He does.

Sinclair: And you worship that kind of God!

Johnston: Yes I worship this kind of God because the challenge of believing it is this, you and I, if we accept our human responsibilities, are given the challenge of being partners with God in trying to do something about war, in trying to do something about famine, in trying to do something about broken homes, in trying to do something about the bloody mess the world is in. I believe that God goes at it through people like you and me and that he has been doing something."

I felt that Gordon still hadn't received an answer to his question about prayer, and frankly I was interested in Dr. Johnston's reply. Like Gordon I have always been intrigued by people's view of prayer. Very often in an interview, even when my guest is talking about an unrelated subject, I'll ask for an opinion on prayer. Almost everyone prays in one way or another. For some it's an outright request for specific things like money, a new job or a car. For others it is a desperate plea for help. "Please don't let this person die" or "Help me out of this mess God and I'll never do it again." Some see prayer as comfortable words passing between friends, bringing a sense of peace and strength. I have heard people describe prayer as gratitude, a simple thank you for some small experience or momentary pleasure. So often has the subject come up in my interviews that I have included several comments on prayer in this book.

I pressed Dr. Johnston for an answer to Gordon's question and he replied, "God answers prayers in a variety of ways, sometimes positively, sometimes negatively, sometimes by withholding the answer for a long time. He answers prayer by working spiritually through me or you or a statesman, a businessman, a trade union worker, or a missionary, or anyone who has integrity and energy."

Gordon thought it must be confusing to have so many gods. He asked Johnston where the God of Islam and the Hebrew God fit into his understanding. The reply was that they were one and the same.

But it was really with the organized church that Gordon took exception. He denied that he had ever attacked the church and I believe this is true.

I have heard Gordon many times on his CFRB radio programme lash out at the hypocrisy he saw in church pronouncements and what he felt to be contradictions in the behaviour of some religious figures. On television and in print he has criticized churches for their wealth in the face of third world poverty and questioned adherence to unprovable beliefs. He has never to my knowledge maliciously attacked a religious individual or advocated the abolition of a church sect. However, his criticism of some of the church's activities has put him on the enemy list of a number of clerics.

I asked Gordon if he thought the church was relevant at all.

"Certainly," he answered, "ceremonially. I think they are very useful in performing marriages, burying the dead, having places for people to meet. I wouldn't abolish the church, but I'd certainly tax it."

Taxes have always been a sore point with Gordon. Many free-enterprising Canadians shout "hallelujah" when he takes off after the government's apparent "soak the working man and then give it away through welfare" policies.

Sinclair: "Now the church is always saying we have to help people. That's part of our problem. People don't stand on their own two feet. It's always 'God help me. Government help me. Give me a hand out here.' Why don't they help themselves?

Johnston: That's all right for you to say Gordon. You're lucky. You're healthy. You're wealthy. You're making money and your money is making money.

Sinclair: Well, don't knock it.

Johnston: But what if you weren't so lucky? Don't we have to help one another? As St. Paul says 'bear one another's burdens and so fulfill the role of Christ.' In other words, it's a Christian thing to help your neighbour.

94

Sinclair: It's also likely a Jewish thing.

Johnston: Of course it is! It's universal. But the Bible also says that a man has to carry his own load, and what a person has to admire about you Gordon is that you don't want to sponge on anyone and you don't want anyone to sponge on you.

Sinclair: Well, I agree with that!

Johnston: But it's instinctive to want to help your neighbour. You don't hit a man when he's down. You lift him up.

Sinclair: But we try to straighten all this out with a thing called income tax.

Johnston: Not quite.

Sinclair: We damn well do!

Johnston: Well I agree with the income tax, don't you?

Sinclair: No I do not! The graduated income tax, in a land that poses as a democracy, absolutely ruins the idea of equality. They tax me more than they tax the average person.

Johnston: That's because you make more.

Sinclair: Certainly it is, but I make it through my own efforts. I worked hard for it. Then they take it away from me. Where's the democracy in that?

Johnston: Well, the democracy is this. From each according to his ability....

Sinclair: That's Karl Marx!

Johnston: All right, all right, to each according to his needs.

Sinclair: You're quoting Marx....

Johnston: What's wrong with that?

Sinclair: I don't want Marx running this country.

Johnston: I don't want him to run it either, but when he speaks something that is true and decent you have to admit it, don't you?

Sinclair: I don't have to admit it at all. The point is, it is not democracy. Don't feed me the idea that democracy is useful and then deny it to me. If they want a universal income tax at the same rate that's fine. Let's all pay fifty per cent, or forty, or twenty, but don't tax somebody ten per cent and the next guy eight. What we have here in Canada is confiscation.

Johnston: I agree, that is confiscation. It would be immoral to take away above a certain percentage.

Sinclair: At what point would you stop?

Johnston: I don't know Gordon. I'm not a trained economist.

Sinclair: It's fifty-four per cent now.

Johnston: Well, that's because you make too much. I'm not in that class.''

Economics came back into the conversation later on in a delightful exchange, which left us all roaring with laughter. Gordon made the fatal error of trying to quote the Bible to prove his point. However, by so doing he endeared himself to all of us laymen, who from time to time have sallied forth, unarmed as it were, into battle with theological expertise.

Sinclair: "Do you believe what Jesus says?

Johnston: Yes, when I'm sure of what he says.

Sinclair: That we have no treasure on earth?

Johnston: Yes, that's right.

Sinclair: It's as easy for a rich man to get into the kingdom of God as for a camel to go through the eye of a needle?

Johnston: Right. It's virtually impossible. Gordon you're in a bad way!

Sinclair: Would you like to have the world run on Christ's economic principles? 'To him who hath shall be given and from him who hath not shall be taken away that which he hath?'

Johnston: Well, in the first place, I deny it was an economic principle. In the second place, I deny your right to throw out a proof text as though a proof text could settle anything. In the third place, your exegesis was wrong because that's not what the parable was teaching. In the fourth place, there are no economic principles in the Christian gospel which can be applied to the modern world.

Sinclair: Me and my big mouth!"

Shortly after the programme aired, the mail started to roll in. Sinclair said it was one of the highest mail responses he had received in his long career in broadcasting. Viewers' reactions were almost evenly split three ways.

A third thought Johnston had won hands down. A third praised Sinclair for pinning that "religious professor against the wall," and the remainder, mostly fundamentalists, lamented the fact that we hadn't pitted Gordon against a "real Christian."

I don't believe these two sincere and caring men were, in essence, very far apart. I remember near the end of the programme I asked them what set of values they lived by. Sinclair said, "My creed is to not deliberately harm anybody, to pay my own way, to meet my own responsibilities, and never to harm anyone else." Johnston said, "My creed is to love my God, to love my neighbour and to help people live meaningfully in a time of rapid change, great perplexity and great suffering."

Barbara Ward

A VOICE IN THE WILDERNESS

You begin with the child. Make it a caring and sharing child. That's the first responsibility of the family.

Lady Jackson, or Barbara Ward as she is more familiarly known, is a frequent *Man Alive* visitor. She has written a great deal to popularize several issues in need of immediate, individual action. She has for example, encouraged millions to learn more about the global effect of our dwindling resources. Her unrelenting challenges to the western world have caused many to take positive steps to correct existing economic and social imbalances.

My last talk with her, a couple of years ago, found her frail from long illness, yet still as feisty and passionate as ever. Her years of travel, lecturing, writing and advising numerous heads of state were taking their toll. But it was cancer that was, slowly but surely, wearing her down.

I recall interviewing her in 1976 at Habitat in Vancouver. Habitat was one in a series of conferences convened by governments of the world to explore the future of life on earth. Stockholm had hosted one on the environment, Bucharest on population growth, Rome on food, Caracas on the sea and its use and Mexico City on the status of women. The official title of Habitat was the United Nations Conference on Human Settlements and Barbara Ward was very much involved.

She had been speaking at the conference about the need for "community" in Canada and around the world. In our conversation I asked her what kind of community she meant.

"I'm talking about a great many communities," she answered, "beginning with the one that is most essential in human life and that is the one formed to protect babies and small children, the family. Unlike animals, our young need about nine or ten years of intensive care. That's the smallest community. Then you have the neighbourhood, the people you live around. Based on settled agriculture it was, for most of human history, our only community. About five thousand years ago, we invented the city and then our community became much more complex.

"There is one more community which has been tremendously strong and that is a little fighting mechanism we invented about five hundred years ago called the nation-state, with its own loyalties, its own boundaries and its own values. The task we now face is to transcend this national sense of 'me, not you' to a planetary society. So much that is essential to the family, the neighbourhood, the nation, to each human being, can only be determined at the planetary level. Food supplies, water, care of the atmosphere, we now see to be planetary issues but we haven't got any sense yet of the larger community."

"Isn't it true," I asked, "that the smaller communities, the neighbourhood, the family seem to be crumbling today? It seems harder for us to get along with each other in small, tight groups."

"We mustn't idealize these small communities," she replied, "or have a view of civilization having been perfect in the past. After all they were composed of human beings and I'm sure included some very awkward customers. Even in the smallest most idyllic neolithic village there were probably aunts whom you couldn't stand.

"Many people leave the village community because there is an oppressiveness in everyone knowing everyone else. I think the crumbling comes from enormously rapid technological change and from sheer scale. The technology which enables you to move much more rapidly and with greater mobility must lessen your rootedness to a particular place. For the first time in the whole history of mankind, people who could never move before, above all agrarian, rural people, find, in this century, they can move and indeed they do."

I had for some time been concerned about the disintegration of small communities. I felt the death of these close knit areas weakened the fabric of our society and, to a large extent, was the cause of our increasing alienation and isolation. I described to Barbara Ward the community in which I was born and raised. It was a cheese-making district with small independent farmer-owned factories dotting the concession roads every few miles. The farmers "drew" their milk to the factory themselves or one farmer, in this case my father, would contract to pick up the milk from ten or twenty neighbouring farms, in a horse drawn wagon and later by truck. Each farmers' name was stencilled on the forty gallon cans used to transport the milk and on the return trip these cans were filled with whey from a large storage tank at the factory. This by-product of the cheese making process was brought back to the farmer and when combined with his own ground grain, became very nutritious pig feed — an early example of recycling. The cheese factory was more than a local enterprise, or cottage industry as they say today, it was a daily meeting place for many in the community: a place to discuss, argue and exchange news.

The school was also a meeting place for the community. Usually only one or two rooms, it was situated conveniently on a corner of a field donated by a local farmer. We walked or bicycled to school and were responsible for keeping the floors and windows clean, and in the winter making sure the furnace was well stoked and fueled from the wood pile provided by our parents. It was the centre for neighbourhood get-togethers, amateur plays, and Christmas concerts. The teacher knew every family in the area and usually boarded with one of them.

The third pivotal point in the community was the church. The Sunday service was a time to come together again and it was a common sight to see neighbours clustered in front of the church long after the final benediction. Baptisms, marriages, and funerals were conducted in these plain, unpretentious buildings and your final resting place was in a plot of land in the churchyard.

The independent factories were the first to go. International cheese companies formed contracts with the larger farm operators and sent their own bulk tanks to pick up the milk at the barn. Interpersonal relations suffered — so did the cheese. Gone was the pride of the local craftsman who could tell at a sniff the true age of his product. What used to be considered "medium" became a plastic tasting "old" after forced curing.

Next, the little red school houses were deemed obsolete. The local boards of education sold them to city buyers who thought it quaint to live in a room with black-board walls or found them ideal for country antique and curio shops. Giant factory-like complexes were constructed many miles from the community and the children unable to walk or cycle to school, were crammed into buses; big yellow vacuum cleaners sucking the kids up along the roadsides. Many country children actually spend more time riding on the bus morning and night than they do in the classroom during the day. Large, impersonal classes, high student-teacher ratios, no responsibility toward the building or facilities increases alienation, apathy, vandalism and dropping out. For the parents the school system became remote and foreign, no longer a part of their community scene.

The same was true of the country church. In the name of efficiency and economy, these oases of comfort and fellowship were boarded up. Parishioners were urged by their presbyteries and dioceses to drive into their nearest towns or cities to attend church. Most did not. Those who did found the surroundings and style of service unfamiliar. The warmth of the small rural Christian "family" with shared needs and concerns was gone.

And so, with the local crafts, schools and churches disappearing for "progress" sake, the community vanished too and we are the poorer for it.

I expressed these thoughts to Barbara Ward and she agreed wholeheartedly.

"It is an unreasoned response to technological change. What you describe in each case is the abandonment of social values for a clear economic cost benefit, and efficiency. I think we are beginning to realize our mistake. Mankind only stumbles into things because it's not able to forsee everything. A lot of these economic costs are based on food versus energy. Your little cheese factory can't stand up to the energy pattern now. Over the next twenty years we are going to have to acquire a new concept of energy use. Petroleum and fossil fuels are going to go up, up, up in price because they are getting scarce. This isn't an Arab plot. It is a fact about society. We've had this absolute drive to bigness, a drive to be enormous and we're beginning to say 'Oh, but we're human.' We need a scale that suits us, not a scale that suits the machine. One of the great awakenings of the twentieth century may be happening now as we see the dangers of big technology which forgets man and we search for really supportive technologies and sciences which give us a community to live in again. This, to me, is one of the more hopeful things that's happening.''

"Should we try to recreate this community?" I asked. "If so what steps should we take?"

"Let's begin where we've gone wrong, which is the big vast, sprawling megalopolitan areas, be it New York, or London, or Paris. The idea of building small communities within them is coming up more strongly. It is all very well to say that a city should be a band of brothers, but a city is a place with very different kinds of people. You need a sort of informal community surveillance. It must be arranged on a visual scale so that Mr. Jones at the corner shop can tell Mrs. Brown that little Johnny is perhaps not behaving the way he should and then you don't have to call in the cops all the time. Vandalism is going up almost in the same ratio as the highrises.''

"But this requires citizen participation and commitment," I said. "We might very well say 'Yes, Barbara Ward is right. This is what I'd like in my area,' but what are the steps one can take?''

"I think one could take an example from a very remarkable citizen participation group, the environmental movement in the United States. It began with a few bodies like the Sierra Clubs and the Audubon Society. They work on a basic form of citizen education which is very often on a one-to-one basis. Everyone who is connected feels an absolute responsibility to get five other people to join in the debate. They may not make converts out of them but the issues are disseminated. They say, 'We're doing this in Bridgeport, now what are you doing in Westchester?' That sort of interchange in an open society like the United States really got the environmental movement off the ground. It's really a case of citizens being convinced enough to stay with it. It's easy to be converted for a week, more difficult for a year and very, very difficult for a lifetime.

"The next step is to get citizen action to influence voters. If your congressman or your member of parliament thinks citizens don't give a damn, he's not going to care, because he doesn't have the time. He's being pressured by everyone, but usually by the big interests. The Americans have a phrase 'money never sleeps.' The citizen is up against something very tough if, for example, he wants to stop a highway from going through. That highway has a whole construction industry behind it. I'm not trying to make bogies out of the construction industry. If they had social guidelines, they'd follow them. It's just that in the

1950's and 1960's the social guideline given to the construction industry was to build roads over anything they could lay their hands on. And who can say the citizen didn't want it that way as he drove around in his station wagon with gas at fifteen cents a gallon.

"You can't completely blame big business, but I am saying that we've got to have social guidelines so that when a citizen goes to his member of parliament he can say, 'Look we citizens have decided that to put a highway straight through this particular community will destroy it. It will give us something we don't want. You have already got half the city under concrete. We don't want anymore.' It's this kind of personal commitment, citizen organization, and intense, continuous, and if necessary, extremely tough lobbying we need. I have a saying I use often 'bite the congressman in the calf.' He will notice after a week."

I suggested that many people would not risk making the changes necessary for the creation of these kind of communities. Everyone may agree that they are desirable, but our own habits, lifestyles and feelings would have to be altered. This gave her the opportunity to criticize our luxurious western mode of living.

"I think twenty-five years, in the developed world, of unashamed and total pursuit of affluence is enough — the colour television, the you owe yourself a holiday in Bermuda stuff, you are not a person of distinction unless you 'own the latest' syndrome. Well, I meet more and more people who have had it up to here, who think it's getting to be, let's be frank, slightly obscene. With the increased price of energy people are making some quite new calculations.

"In North America between forty and fifty per cent of the energy that is paid for is wasted. We drive these greedy, guzzling machines and there is no need for such waste. We shall have to begin to tax ourselves. We shall have to begin to have automatic means of sharing with the developing world. We've got to look at our diets. The American Medical Association, which I would not regard as a highly radical organization, has told the American people that they eat one-third too much protein in the form of meat. We should adopt a simpler diet. These are not the kinds of things that should scare people stiff and cause the destruction of their way of life. It's just a matter of becoming less selfish, more sharing. We must have a base so that everyone has the minimum. We must also think about an upper limit."

After other programmes with Barbara Ward viewers wrote letters appreciative of her remarks and concern. The only criticism

I ever heard was of her idealism. Some who wrote thought her suggestions for change impractical. I decided to push her to a more specific position on what the individual could actually do. "You've been called an idealist. Can we have some practical guidelines as to where to start? What do we do?"

"You begin with the child. Make it a caring and sharing child. That's the first responsibility of the family. It's a little more difficult now that families are small because in the old days you jolly well had to share. My earliest memories were of my mother sort of slapping me over the ear because I was trying to pinch my brother's toys. She would say 'You are not to behave like that. You two are going to share and what's more you're very, very lucky.' From the very beginning I had it drummed into me that I was fortunate and that I wasn't owed anything. Of course we didn't have television telling us constantly that we owe ourselves everything. That's why parents must make the extra effort to let children in the wealthy countries know that they are the elite. They are the children of the palace. They are the princes of the realm. Not enough feel like that. They are brought up with so many wants that they forget about other people's needs. So that's where we begin.

"Then, in our educational system, let there be a planetary dimension. Let's not have just national history but the extraordinary adventure of the human race. Begin with our evolutionary beginnings. Let's see how organic life came to be on this planet. Explain that we could not have organic life at all until we had the shield of the ocean and the shield of the atmosphere. Then they would understand some of the horrors going on today like the casual introduction of nuclear breeder reactors inside the biosphere. We are putting inside the biosphere what for three-fourths of organic life on this planet is totally destructive. It's blasphemy to do it in the casual, commercial way that we do.

"Let's have the children learn something of the evolution of our whole organic system of life. Some kids now think that milk comes from bottles and food comes from cans and the whole marvelous system of our living, acting, working biosphere is completely forgotten. We should teach them a sense of love and respect for our natural system and that we shouldn't so aggressively manipulate things for our own purposes.

"Science has given us such instruments of power that we've sometimes forgotten its instruments of knowledge. The instruments of knowledge, particularly through biology, tell us to treat our planet with respect. Treat your own body with respect. Don't

103

waste. Don't muck things up. An example is the non-returnable bottle or can. It breeds a throw-away mentality in our children and leads to disrespect. If they do not respect their environment they will not respect each other.

"There's a remarkable town planner named Colin Buchanan who said, 'I hate squalor. It reminds me of violence.' And he is right. It is because we have squalid cities that we have violent kids.

"So, after education comes community. What are you going to give them to live in? Studies in both Europe and North America show that when you put families into these vast tower blocks without a sense of who or where they are, you get vandalism and violence. Builders have to make so much money out of each plot that they go up eighty floors. So, another element in community control is land values."

This, for me, brought up the whole question of home ownership. I remember back in the 1950's buying my first home, albeit a modest one, for $7,000.00 with a $500.00 down payment and a mortgage of 4½%. With today's land values, building costs and high interest rates it's virtually impossible for a young person to start out in his own home. "I don't think my kids are going to be able to own their own home," I said. "I don't see how they can possibly afford it."

"I think you've put your finger on one of the great destroyers of community. We must get control over basic land values. All the incremental value that is put on land, because they want to use it for a city or industrial site, must come back to the community. But we don't put communities first. We put roads first, or cars first, or industries first or defense, defense, defense. It's a shame that the thing people need most, the community, isn't a very big priority.

"When people come to the conviction that, say not less than ten per cent of our gross national product, should be used for the building and improvement of communities, then they should form an association of Canadian cities and lobby until they get the money. First the caring citizen, then other people who care, forming themselves into lobbies that stay with it, election after election, fighting for communities with basic services, with neighbourliness, with love. What could be better? What could be more human?"

I always find it interesting to interview a person several times over a span of years. Some people change their views completely, some remain static and thus become dated. I have found that most radical thinkers, critics of society and prophets of doom tend to mellow over the years. Perhaps this is because they become weary with "crying in the wilderness" or maybe advancing age brings its own tempering influence. Once, in the early 1970's, when I talked with Barbara Ward I accused her of writing and speaking in a desperate tone. She thought about this for awhile.

"Am I desperate? Am I not desperate? Let me see. I think I'm less desperate than I was. When I look back now at my own writing and at what I was thinking, so much then was written from an adversary position. I was with the generation of the concentration camp. I was in the generation of Stalinism. One of my best friends, Jan Masarik, was murdered in Prague in 1948. He was made to jump out of a window. To say, at that time, that communism wasn't a threat in Europe, was nonsense. Of course it was a threat and therefore one was writing in this adversary position. What has changed is that every system is in the same boat now and the problems we confront are planetary problems. They are problems in which sharing, responsibility, the new science, new insights into ecology, all point in the same direction. Reform based on being an adversary will not solve these problems. We need reform based upon the fact that we have got, as a human species, to find a way of living in the technological order without destroying our planet."

While Barbara Ward may have mellowed in her manner of writing she could still be pugnacious and testy in personal confrontation especially if she felt you were attacking her favourite institution, the Christian church. A devout Roman Catholic, she has always spoken out on behalf of the church and defended it against all argument. I found out how sensitive she was on the subject. Although it was a specific remark that caused Barbara Ward to explode on camera, I realize now looking back over the transcripts of the interview that the tension had been building for several minutes.

We were discussing the need for sacrifice and what role the Christian community might play in the promotion of a more equitable life for all. She said she would like to see the church take a stand on increased taxation of wealthy interests and more support for basic minimum wage laws. When she said that the church should make a statement about the justice of taxation, I answered, "I find it hard to believe the church will make any statement about taxation, when they are so against taxing their own property."

"Well, this may be an issue, but you have to look at what the properties are being used for."

"But will anyone listen to the churches' pronouncements? You are being quoted in pulpits around the world but I wonder if it's being taken seriously. Does the average parishioner, when he goes to church, get upset about the state of the world?"

"I think it's enormously difficult to generalize. If you're asking me whether, within the Christian community in the broadest sense, there are not more people concerned with the issues of justice, basic solidarity and planetary survival, I would say there is. We are western and post-colonial and the church was part of the period when we went around the world taking everything we could get. But I have a feeling that in the re-evaluation of the conscience of the west, that same re-evaluation is going on within the church itself."

I reminded her that earlier in our conversation she had accused the western powers of only letting our "leftovers trickle down to the poor nations." I suggested the church could be criticized for the same attitude. It was the way I worded my statement that brought her half out of the studio chair, eyes snapping.

"The churches have done this too," I said. "Over the years we gave the poor nations our worn-out clothing and we sent over our spinster missionaries."

"I say!" she shouted, "I will fight you to the death. I really think you've made a statement that I find shocking. You said 'spinster' missionary and you mention it next to old clothing? How could you? This is where *you* need re-evaluation. You are speaking of a sisterhood which includes some of the noblest souls I have ever known. They have gone out to serve in education, in health, in saving babies. It wasn't just colonialism. No, it was not colonialism. It was 'let's go where the need is worst.' And it was not our old clothing!"

"But they went out with strings attached," I continued. "They went out to convert the 'heathen.' They said, 'We will help you if you accept our God!'"

"Yes."

"Isn't that true?"

"Certainly."

"Why should they go to the poor with strings attached? Jesus never did. He just went where the need was."

"Yes, but a great many of these dear sisters whom you call spinsters, and couple them with old clothing, did exactly that when they got there. If they took Christ with them it wasn't to thrust down people's throats. It was to give him in their service.

Now, I'm sorry, but you made me just boil at that point."

When she mentioned "dear sisters" I realized Barbara Ward thought I had been referring to Catholic nuns in my remark about spinsters. It certainly sounded so. I had, however, a different image in mind throughout the discussion. My complaint was certainly not with the teacher or the medical missionary, or the well-driller but with the old time Bible pounding, up-tight Protestant "converter," saving "heathen" souls by covering up their nakedness.

I realized she had misunderstood me, so I apologized.

"I'm sorry."

"No, it's alright, I'm glad you said it. It's a sign that we lay people must do some re-evaluation."

She started to smile, so no damage had been done to our relationship. I thought that before she had fully recovered might be a good time to press a more personal question.

"You talk about the affluent west, the privileged. This means you are also talking about Barbara Ward and her society."

"Yes."

"Is it a problem for you?"

"Of course."

"Do you feel you share this guilt?"

"Naturally. I belong to the most privileged minority in human history, privileged in every conceivable way. To live through this for sixty some years and have so little to show for this obligation is a shaming thing."

I assured her that she had done more than most of us to fulfill our obligation here on earth and urged her once again to give some sort of guideline to follow in our attempt to live more fully and more humbly.

"I think everyone has to find their own first step but I would suggest finding near you someone with a problem; someone who is in a situation of the greatest possible constraint and see what you personally can do about it. Then secondly, we could make sure that in all the pressure we can exert as citizens, local, regional and national, we put the needs of the dispossessed first not last as they now are. And third, that we add to our lives the dimension of living on a planet that we must share as a human species, and create within that planet the kind of civility and sense of justice we must achieve as an imperative to survival.

"Everyone can examine their own way of life and ask whether or not they are devoting all their energies to just themselves or their immediate families. There's a toast in Yorkshire, where I come from, which goes:

> Here's to me and my son John
> His wife, my wife
> Us four, no more.

If we live like that I don't think the planet will survive.

"I do however, feel that the time for re-examination is becoming clearer with the younger generation as we face more pressing problems, new constraints and environmental imperatives.

"I'm not sure about this because memories and particularly images come and go so quickly these days, including yours and mine, my dear. Still, I think the image of the earth seen from the moon is a compelling one. It is very small. It is very beautiful. It is worth keeping. In environmental terms we're behaving stupidly in the use of resources but I'm so grateful that some things are renewable, like wine for instance. And I'm so glad there are all kinds of people saying, 'What can I do now, immediately? Tell me and I'll get on with it.' "

"Tell me Barbara Ward, do we have time?"

"We've got all the time we've got — which is a lifetime."

We may not be able to share much more of Barbara Ward's "lifetime." For some time now she has been steadily weakening in her struggle against cancer. When she dies we will have lost a brilliant and incisive prophet and one of the greatest defenders this planet ever had.

Hans Kung

LONG LIVE
THE KUNG

One cannot detect a trace of honesty or
Christian fraternity in them; on the contrary,
they breathe the spirit of the Inquisition!

When Father Hans Kung, the controversial Roman Catholic theologian, was recently censured by the Vatican and removed from his teaching position at Tubingen University in Germany, few who followed his stormy career were surprised. Nor were they surprised at Kung's reaction. Following his suspension and his citation as "uncatholic," Kung wrote: "Many distortions and untruths have been disseminated in the past three months particularly by the official church. You know the conditions under which my *missio canonica* was taken away from me cannot be called just and fair. One cannot detect a trace of honesty or Christian fraternity in them; on the contrary, they breathe the spirit of the Inquisition!"

He added, "What is at issue here is nothing more and nothing less than the direction which the Catholic Church intends to take in the coming decade."

Fifty-two year old Kung has been investigated and "under review" by the Vatican since the 1950's, but until now has received only "stern warnings." During this time he has challenged the official position of the Roman Catholic Church in a number of very sensitive areas.

He was admonished by the Doctrinal Congregation in 1975 for his views on the infallibility of the Pope. He advocated optional celibacy for priests; the election of the Pope, not by the college of cardinals, but by a body of clergy and laity representing the whole church, and he called for a "correction" of the encyclical *Humanae Vitae* on birth control. He called the declaration by the Vatican's Doctrinal Congregation barring the ordination of women "an example of how you cannot use the New Testament," claiming that, "in his time Jesus was far ahead of today's church in regard to women." He also dismissed the question of the virgin birth of Jesus as unimportant. "Jesus' divine sonship," said Kung, "is not dependent on the virgin birth. Neither Jesus' sonship nor God's fatherhood can be understood in terms of biological origin. There is no incompatibility between birth from God and human procreation." For Kung, Easter is much more central to the Christian faith than Christmas.

Despite pressure from the Vatican and criticism from fellow theologians Kung continued to write best-selling books and widely read articles for both the religious and secular press.

In October of 1979 Father Kung wrote a long article for the Paris newspaper *Le Monde* giving a critical evaluation of Pope John Paul II's first year as pontiff. This may have been the last straw from the Vatican's point of view. In December, the Sacred Congregation for the Doctrine of the Faith, formerly known as The Office of the Holy Inquisition, stated in part, "Professor Hans Kung, in his writings, has departed from the integral truth of Catholic faith and therefore he can no longer be considered a Catholic theologian nor function as such in a teaching role."

The discussions prior to the final censure were held *in absentia* causing Kung to criticize the Vatican for being "shrouded in secrecy." His reaction was to denounce the Vatican as "scandalous." He told a West German television audience, "I am ashamed of my church."

Reaction was swift from both clergy and laity. Dean Wolfgang Bartholomaeous and eight other faculty members at the University of Tubingen said, in a statement supporting their colleague, "We see heavy damages for the believability of the church in today's society and for the freedom of theology in research and teaching."

The World Council of Churches in Geneva said that the Vatican's ban on Father Kung could hinder ecumenical talks aimed at removing doctrinal differences between Christians.

Generally, Canada's theologians rushed to Kung's support. Gregory Baum, professor of religious studies at the University of Toronto and a theologian of international reputation, often in disagreement with Kung, said that ordering Kung removed from his teaching post in Tubingen was not the way to solve theological controversies. "We need good arguments and discussions not authoritarianism."

Jesuit theologian David Stanley of Regis College, Toronto, described the situation as "ominous," claiming there has to be some kind of academic freedom within the church. Harry McSorley a theologian at the University of Toronto's St. Michael's College, said the Vatican action could make the most interesting case since Martin Luther.

A group of twenty prominent Canadian Roman Catholic lay people, including Conservative MP Douglas Roche and Ottawa Mayor Marion Dewart, protested to the Vatican. Six executive clergy of the Anglican Church of Canada sent an open letter to Rome accusing the Sacred Congregation of authoritarianism and asking it to reconsider.

Gerald Emmett Cardinal Carter, Archbishop of Toronto, however, defended Rome's action and said that the *magisterium* had not only the right, but the duty to define and defend what it understands to be essential to the truth of the Gospel. "If then, as maintained, Hans Kung has held and taught positions that cast doubt upon the divinity of Christ and that repudiate the Church's understanding of infallibility, why should one be surprised if Church authorities declare that for doing so he is no longer to be considered, in an official sense, a Catholic theologian?"

In April of this year it was announced that Kung would remain a professor at Tubingen University. He said his status had been resolved and he would no longer be responsible to the Catholic theology department. "I think it is an honorable solution," said Kung.

Whether you agree with Hans Kung or not no one disputes his brilliance as a contemporary religious thinker and as a communicator able to reach the layman. Too many theologians write to impress other theologians and the ensuing dialogue holds little interest for, or relevance to, the man in the street.

I first met Hans Kung in 1971 when *Man Alive* arranged a discussion between Kung and Harry McSorley, who had criticized Kung's book, *Infallible? An Inquiry!* A studio audience was invited to join in that discussion.

In his book, Kung challenged the infallibility of the Pope, a doctrine adopted at the first Vatican Council over one hundred years ago. The book received a stern "cease and desist" warning from the Vatican and a rash of criticism.

Karl Rahner's criticism was the most notable and surprising. Rahner, a fellow German theologian, has likely done more than any other man to bring Catholic theology up to date, but he took exception to Kung shaking what he considered one of the foundations of Christian belief. He responded by writing an article attacking the book. This action began a debate between the two which attracted international attention. Theologians of all faiths began to take part. A collaboration of four North American theologians resulted in a further publication, *The Infallibility Debate*. Gregory Baum and Harry McSorely teamed with Richard McBrien, a professor of theology from Boston, and George Lindbeck, a Lutheran theologian from Yale.

In *The Infallibility Debate*, McSorley criticized Kung for demanding proof of the Pope's infallibility. He also disagreed with Kung's conclusion that the *Humanae Vitae* encyclical was a significant "error" by the Roman Catholic Church.

In front of the audience in our *Man Alive* studios, the debate continued. While it was not a heated discussion between Kung and McSorley, his former student, it gave Canadians a rare chance to see and hear a world renowned theologian speak unequivocally and in understandable language. Kung was then in the middle of a world tour. He was reluctant to admit that the infallibility debate was at the forefront of his current popularity. Instead, he viewed the question of the Pope's infallibility as merely a symptom of a much more important disease, the disease of estrangement. He said, "The main thing is the Christian message today, the hope that we can have a church nearer to God and nearer to the people and where the people are not constantly hindered because we cannot correct our mistakes."

Kung's support of the Catholic Church is basic and never wavering. He is convinced that the church will survive because of the truth of the Gospel. "We are still a church. It goes on and on, not because we make no mistakes, no errors, but, as I've stated, despite all our errors and through all our errors."

The infallibility decision of Vatican I left no room for sociological interpretation. Kung said: "(It is) stated very clearly that the first man to speak about papal infallibility was around 1300. He was condemned because of his doctrine. The first Popes were embarrassed by this doctrine. There are just so many historical difficulties."

As the discussion continued it became more evident that faith was going to play a large part in each man's argument. Kung asked for biblical proof of infallibility. McSorely had none, but maintained that church history laid a firm basis for this belief and that two thousand years of experience and decision-making could not be wrong. He asked Kung, "We might be wrong?"

"Yes," said Kung, "It's always possible, yes."

McSorely countered, "And the church, for two thousand years, could have been in error?"

"Fortunately it was not."

Here Kung was content to rely on his faith to back up his support of Roman Catholicism as a whole. In the peripheral issues he was willing to speak in logical terms but when discussing the basis of Christianity he re-entered the realm of faith. When McSorely challenged this change in stance Kung admitted there was no proof of the truth of the Gospels, but said there were "reasons" to believe, much as McSorely had maintained there were "reasons" to believe in the concept of infallibility.

The need for a democratic religion seemed much on Kung's mind. He asserted that this was a popular wish and indeed this was one of the points with which McSorely was in some agreement. Kung stated that the Pope was "the only survivor of the French Revolution." The papacy itself, in other words, was the only contemporary example of the ruling class as it existed before being overthrown in the eighteenth century.

The scope of the discussion widened to include the far-ranging issues of celibacy, birth control and inter-church relations. The conflicts within the church are of a very serious nature. Kung points out "If Pope Paul would have said at the beginning of his synod, 'I think it is now a time to accept a minimum of married men to the priesthood,' probably ninety per cent of his bishops would have said, 'yes, we very much agree.' But because they know he hasn't they do not speak out."

This is a further alienating factor in that individuals in local parishes are using their own consciences as a guide and very often going against the official interpretation. Many Catholic priests provide birth control information to their parishoners or give communion to Protestants, proving to a great degree that, at least in their opinion, the Pope was wrong in the banning of these practices.

I let Kung and McSorely debate for about three quarters of an hour, then invited the audience to join in. They were friendly but Kung seemed defensive and testy. I thought that he, like most professors, was more used to one way lecturing than two way dialogue. The combination of Kung, McSorely, and the audience, did, however, make a memorable *Man Alive*.

The response to this programme, plus the fact that Kung kept writing succinct and challenging works, convinced us to have him back on *Man Alive*.

The opportunity came in 1977 following the tremendous success of Kung's book, *On Being A Christian*. It had been a best seller in Germany for over a year and its translation was sweeping the English speaking world.

He agreed to a *Man Alive* interview. This time we would go to him. Bebenhausen, where the programme was filmed, is a tiny village in Germany, three kilometers south of Tubingen. Nestled in a forest valley, it appears at first sight like a scene out of the twelfth century. In fact, the monastery where we set up our lights and cameras was founded in 1190 and at one time was a hunting lodge for the Wittenburg Kings. Here, you are transported back in time to a picture book Germany.

We were seated at a thick oak table beneath huge iron chandeliers and surrounded by stone walls covered with ancient trophies of the hunt. It was a unique setting for a conversation with one of today's leading, and most controversial, theologians.

I remembered a comment of Kung's on that earlier visit to Toronto: "No one has ever accused me of having an inferiority complex." And indeed he had seemed brash, even arrogant at times, engendered perhaps by the criticism and denouncement that had come from many of his colleagues and from within his own beloved church. While still self assured, he seemed more relaxed and casual. We spent the afternoon before the interview in his comfortable Tubingen home sipping sherry and discussing possible areas to be covered the next day.

Despite being ordered by Pope Paul to stop spreading views contrary to Roman doctrine in 1975 he had stood by his beliefs and continued his writing. A total of twenty-four books had preceded his latest work. He told us that he felt bound to write for, "those who believe but feel insecure," those who once believed "but are not satisfied with their unbelief" and those outside the church who are unwilling to approach "the fundamental questions of human existence with mere feelings, personal prejudices and apparently plausible explanations."

During the filming I asked him why it was so important to write *On Being A Christian.* Didn't all faiths really deal with the same question?

He said that questions such as "who are we?" "where are we going" "what are the norms in my life?" might be identical in all religions, but the answers were not quite the same.

"I think it's very difficult," he said, "to go for instance the way of Buddha and the way of Jesus of Nazareth at the same time. You cannot be a monk and go the way of aestheticism and still go the way of a man who lived together with the people. We must never despise the others, or say we alone have 'the truth,' but I think we have a specific truth."

He emphasized that it was Jesus Christ that made Christianity "Christian." The other faiths lacked the vision of self, of man and society, that he found in Christianity.

I asked him why being a humanist wasn't enough. He responded with a theory he had developed.

"I believe that a Christian can be a more radical humanist, in the sense that he is able to integrate the more negative side of human life. It is easy, as humanists do, to affirm everything that is good, true, nice and beautiful. The problem today is to integrate that which is not so good, to account for the problems and the suffering of the world. Here I think a Christian who knows what the Cross means can go deeper and be a better humanist than the secular one."

When I asked him to describe this Christ, who meant so much to him, he answered primarily in negatives telling me what Christ wasn't.

"For many people Christ is just a pious figure. They know him from pictures, not from scripture. It is important to see that he does not fit into a certain scheme. He was not a priest. He was a layman and the leader of a lay movement. He was not a social revolutionary or a man from Moral Rearmament who just tried to be moral in his life. He associated with very immoral people. He was closer to God than the priests and closer to the world than the aesthetics. He was more moral than the moralists and more revolutionary than the revolutionaries."

Part of the opposition Hans Kung encountered with the Vatican came from his comments about Christ's divinity and Virgin Birth. I wanted to hear him, first hand, express his views on these essential issues.

"We have to be careful that we don't confuse Jesus with the

Father. They are really different persons. Jesus himself is the revelation of God. We can see him as the Son of God but we mustn't forget he was a real human being. The Virgin Birth is certainly not central to the Christian message. Mark doesn't mention the Virgin Birth. John doesn't mention it. St. Paul speaks of Jesus being 'born of woman.' It can be a symbol to express a basic truth, the sonship of God; an expression of his origin. His significance and his importance are not just found in history but come from God himself. Today we do not need to interpret it in the biological way, but in the theological way.''

"Wouldn't we understand Jesus more," I asked, "if we ignored such things as the Virgin Birth and the miracles and those stories of his life which could be considered as myth. Wouldn't we be better off if we just concentrated on Jesus the man?''

"It would be possible of course," said Kung, "just to have a historical report, but I think these legendary narratives explain a great deal. I don't think it is good to rationalize everything. Man needs symbols, because he is not just pure reason. Man needs to see, to imagine. If, for example, we were to reduce the Old Testament to just principles, I think it would be boring. In the story of Jesus in the New Testament we need everything we have, but we must interpret it. We shouldn't take historically what is only symbolic. We have to see the spirit and not just the letter.''

The resurrection, on the other hand, Kung feels is far more important. When I asked him if it was an historical event he said he would prefer to call it a "real event.''

"Historical means that it is set in time and space and that you could practically photograph it. As a matter of fact since we have so many nice pictures by Raphael and others a lot of people think in such a way. I think the basic truth of Easter is that Jesus did not die into nothingness, but into God. We believe then, that we too do not just die into nothingness, but into this first and last reality called God. It is very basic for the New Testament. As a matter of fact if they hadn't believed in the resurrection, nothing would have been written down of his message or of his suffering. With the resurrection everything he did before became important and was justified.''

When Kung's *On Being A Christian* was published it stirred up new controversies. He was called, by some, a non-Catholic, told to "become a Protestant," and accused of having lost his faith. The German bishops found many points to be "less than orthodox" and have repeatedly warned him to correct these "errors." He feels that constructive answers to fundamental

116

questions are required, not denunciations. When he told me that his next book was "proving the Existence of God," I commented that if he completed this there would be nothing left for him to write.

"Theology is never at an end," he replied. "I would like to have more practical dialogue with scientists, with physicists, biologists, sociologists and I shall keep trying to be in contact with people and explain what God means to us today."

Kung's contact with today's world keeps his theology fresh and relevant. His manner of thinking and writing make his views accessible to everyone whether they agree or not.

One can understand why, when Professor Kung was under heavy pressure from the Vatican and violent attacks by fellow theologians, his Tubingen students marched around the five hundred year old University chanting "Long live the Kung."

Robert MacLure

THEY'LL TELL ME
WHEN THE
TREAD'S GONE

*You are here for a purpose and that is
to serve your fellow man. When you do that,
you also serve your God.*

In January of 1970 we suddenly realized that Dr. Robert Mac-Lure's term of office as moderator of the United Church of Canada would be ending in a few weeks. Unless we booked a studio and arranged for an interview quickly this remarkable man would likely be off to God knows where and we'd miss our chance. We heard rumours of Borneo.

Over the years I had spent a good many hours with MacLure at conferences, seminars, panel discussions and travelling across Canada. Many an anxious moment was spent at airports wondering whether he would actually board. He refused to pay full fare since he was entitled to the Senior Citizen discount and consequently ended up on stand-by. While I am sure this saved the church a considerable amount of money, it caused a great deal of frustration for those planning meetings or appearances at the other end of the trip.

We finally managed to get MacLure and a studio together on an evening in the middle of January which is a minor miracle in itself.

It is customary to book studios at least six weeks in advance. There are an incredible number of details to arrange before a programme can be produced. A television crew consists of approximately fourteen people. All of these people must be present and all their equipment must be available before a studio can be booked, thus the need for advanced planning. The process of scheduling facilities begins a full year before any projected need arises. In this case we were able to beg exactly half an hour of tape time to do an interview which would eventually run twenty-seven minutes and thirty seconds. An hour or more is usually allowed for an interview of this nature so that editing can take out any mistakes or weak spots. This day there would be no such luxury. Every question and answer had to be relevant and to the point. The opening and closing would also be recorded at this time. This too is unusual. These finer points of production are usually executed the day before the show is broadcast. This allows a better perspective on what is said in an interview as well as the possible insertion of any topical material which may have come to light in the interim.

It was also no easy task to arrange for MacLure's presence on such short notice.

He was undoubtedly one of the busiest moderators the United Church ever had. He found it very difficult to say no to any request and consequently travelled the country at a hectic pace speaking at anniversary services, service clubs, and hundreds of meetings. Once, when we were both at a conference in Banff, I casually mentioned that I was attending the final service of a small rural church in Ontario on the following Sunday. It was being closed for lack of funds, after one hundred and twenty years.

"I wish I could be there," said MacLure. "I would like to reassure and comfort the congregation if I could. Say, you have a tape recorder there, could you record a few words from me and take it to them?"

I assured him I could and with no preparation he grasped the microphone and proceeded to give a warm, sincere and effective message to a congregation saddened by the loss of its old church. He would often by-pass invitations to Canada's more prestigious parishes to appear at remote church gatherings of only a dozen or so of the faithful, because he realized they never had the opportunity to see and talk to the highest official of their church.

People found it very easy to relate to MacLure. He looked and sounded like a simple country doctor. He cared little for deep theological discussions, preferring to expound the simpler, more basic tenets of his faith. Living so long with Hindus, Moslems and Buddhists seemed to have blurred their philosophy with his own deep-felt Christian convictions and he epitomized the best aspects of them all.

To him, service to others was what it was all about. He often voiced his embarrassment at members of his own profession. "Take a look at the towns and cities across the country. The largest homes in the best areas are usually owned by the doctors. Becoming wealthy out of human suffering is an abomination. Every doctor or nurse should spend at least a year in countries with desperate health conditions. Most of their time in Canada is spent treating people whose problems are caused by eating too much and depression which is attributable to their affluence."

He constantly told people, "You are here for a purpose and that is to serve your fellow man. When you do that, you also serve your God."

MacLure was, as they say, "good press." The first colour programme ever broadcast on the CBC in 1966 was a documentary on MacLure in India. During his term as moderator he grabbed headlines and air space with his pithy, controversial and sometimes shocking statements. Though certainly sincere in his beliefs, he had a flair for the dramatic and his reputation for calling a spade a spade made him a darling of the media. Before the interview I gave much thought to the best method of keeping MacLure succinct. I knew if I gave him his head the interview would result in a detailed accounting of lengthy anecdotes garnered during his incredible career as a medical missionary in India and China. As interesting as the stories might be, many had been heard before and there simply was no time. I was about to start a race with the studio clock.

As we settled in our chairs and the countdown began I leaned over and said, "Bob, when I ask you about prayer, don't go into the story about the Parsee in the desert at dawn. And we simply won't have time for an account of the pickled body parts on that slow boat to China in the 1930's." He assured me he wouldn't digress from the topics at hand, and we were off. Twenty seven minutes later I asked, "Bob we have thirty seconds left, what advice would you give the incoming moderator?"

"Well, besides wishing him success, I would urge him to let

the people know there is no such thing as a steady place for the church. There's no such thing as a routine part to be played by the church. The church is forever changing, and he should always keep the pot boiling."

A pot boiler is certainly an apt description of MacLure himself. It was no secret that some officials at the United Church head office wished fervently that he would keep a lower profile. When I asked him once about clashes with church officials he said that they were actually very charitable. "I suspect the hierarchy may have been given a briefing before I arrived. I think they felt well, here is this crazy man. He's been in the east, probably out in the sun without a hat, and he's liable to do strange things."

I had seen MacLure in the presence of young people. Here I think was his greatest contribution as moderator. Certainly MacLure himself considered it the most happy and gratifying part of his term in office. He visited one hundred and one high schools across Canada during these two and one half years.

His tendency to do the unexpected endeared him to young people who had come to expect a more sober approach from the church and certainly from the office of moderator.

At one gathering in Calgary, attended by over a thousand people of all ages, MacLure was the main evening speaker. I had given an address in the afternoon and was staying to introduce MacLure after dinner. The microphone in the auditorium had given me problems most of the day and I complained several times about its poor quality. As the moment arrived I introduced, with proper dignity and solemnity "the distinguished moderator of the United Church of Canada, Dr. Robert MacLure."

Down the aisle he came to the gasps of the crowd. Instead of the traditional black moderator's gown, he was wearing denim coveralls, a hard construction hat and carrying a screw driver, a monkey wrench and a hammer. He marched up to the microphone, which of course by now was working beautifully, gave it a couple of sharp taps and explained to me "You see Roy, if something goes wrong with the system, fix it. Too many stand around and complain. It's a waste of time. The problems of this world will never be solved by complaining or 'letting George do it.' We have to take action on our own."

With this visual demonstration, his good humoured chastisement of me and the crowd in the palm of his hand he then doffed his hard hat and proceeded with a stirring address on the need for personal commitment to an active faith.

MacLure was a breath of fresh air after the hand wringing and self-abuse the church underwent in the 1960's. His practical views and infectious optimism gave me, and I'm sure many other Canadians, a more hopeful perspective on our times.

The concerns of organized religion seem almost petty when placed alongside MacLure's world view gained from a wealth of practical experience.

The question of church union, for example, while a hot item in Canada during the late 1960's and early 1970's, was something he had taken for granted in the mission field.

"Throughout the world," he told me, "the co-operation that has existed is marvellous. In India we had Protestant missionaries working with Hindu Indians drilling wells for thirsty people with a drill rig that was purchased by Catholics. This is ecumenism. And you know the water that came up was completely non-denominational."

He took a rather jaundiced view of the youth protest movement in North America. "I've seen protests by people who were being denied their political rights. I've seen protests of young people ready to die for their beliefs. Here it's sort of a protest between cokes. To me a coca-cola protest is pretty small bubbles."

He also had little patience for the Canadian penchant for criticizing America at a time when it was very popular to do so.

"While we must be interested in what is going on there, we should not adopt this holier than thou attitude. We should realize what they are facing, then look inwards to ourselves and see if we can learn from them. In the problem of race relations, for example, I'm surprised we haven't learned, from their problems, the depth of our unfair treatment of our own Indians, Eskimo and Métis.

"I'm surprised too, when we are part of the American industrial machine, that we are still satisfied with the strike as a way of solving industrial disputes. I think it is one of the crudest things that's been developed since man came down from the trees. There must be some better way of regulating the relations between two groups of people."

In a time of decreasing church membership and a questioning of traditonal values Eastern mysticism attracted a number of Canadians. I asked MacLure to comment on this.

"Well, I see this interest in eastern mysticism as a very superficial thing in Canada. I have the greatest respect for it when it's sincere and I have seen it practiced for many years and count many mystics among my friends. But here, if you put on a Nehru

122

jacket and grow a beard, that's about all there is to it. Eastern mysticism is a great respecter of life, so that the mystics in the countries where I have lived have to be vegetarians. He will not carve up and eat the bodies of dead animals. And to hear a man talk about mysticism here then wolf down a hamburger or wear animal hide on his feet, one wonders just how far his beliefs go."

Man Alive caught up with Dr. MacLure again in December of 1972. This time he was on the Island of Borneo in Malaysia serving with his wife Amy at a mission hospital among the Dayaks.

As vibrant and outrageous as ever he gave no indication of slowing down. When asked when he was going to retire he answered "As long as there is tread on the tire you keep rolling along. Perhaps you take the back roads instead of the raceways, but you don't stop. It's really up to the people I work with. They'll tell me when the tread is gone."

Mother Teresa

GOD IN ACTION

There is a poverty of the spirit, a hunger
in the soul. A plate of rice or a loaf
of bread isn't everything.

No religious figure in the world today receives more respect or appreciation than Agnes Gonxha Bojaxhiu, known universally as Mother Teresa of Calcutta. This tiny, somewhat wizened seventy year old woman, has been canonized by the media as "a living saint," and inspires reverence and awe wherever she goes.

I first met her in the spring of 1976. By this time she was famous throughout the world as founder of the Missionaries of Charity, a congregation approved by the Vatican in 1950 and now numbering 1,500 sisters and 200 brothers. Their calling is the running of havens for the dying, leprosariums and children's homes around the world.

They work with the poorest of the poor, the rejected, the diseased and the dying. Mother Teresa has won an array of awards and honours: the Nobel Peace Prize, the first Pope John XXIII Peace Prize, India's Order of the Lotus, the British Templeton

Award, the Albert Schweitzer Prize and many others.

With every appearance on *Man Alive*, viewers responded enthusiastically and asked for more. Although she has reached celebrity status, she shuns the media and says giving interviews is the biggest sacrifice of her life.

Mother Teresa hates to leave her poor and dying in Calcutta to travel abroad, either to raise money or accept awards, but she realizes this too is part of the cross she bears. She is genuinely embarrassed when told she is a "saint" and quite impervious to the accolades of an adoring public.

I was in England when Mother Teresa was awarded the Templeton Prize for "progress in religion." She said the award itself meant very little but that the money would be useful in her work with the dying. As the audience began to leave, one of her co-workers asked where she had put the money she had received. She didn't know. A search of the auditorium found the cheque for £34,000 lying on a chair in a corner of the room.

Mother Teresa was born in Skopje, Yugoslavia in 1910 and as a young girl became interested in India through letters read in school from Yugoslav Jesuits working in the Calcutta Archdiocese. At eighteen she joined the Irish branch of Loreto nuns who also worked in Calcutta and made her final vows in 1937. She taught geography to Bengali girls at St. Mary's High School in Calcutta, later becoming principal. The girls were from comfortable homes and the contrast between the school room and the wretched slums next door was immense. She received what she describes as a "call, within a call," since she was already a nun, to work for the poor and dying in the city on September 19, 1946. Her request was approved by Rome and in August 1948 she changed from the Loreto habit to her now familiar white sari with blue trim. She opened her first slum school just before Christmas. In the spring of the following year she began accepting recruits to help with the work. Many were former students from St. Mary's.

The number of recruits grew and today Mother Teresa and her Missionaries of Charity live in a large, sombre house at 54A Lower Circular Road, Calcutta. Life is hard. There are no amenities to compensate for the wretched work in which they are involved. They live little better than the poor they serve. Mother Teresa lives as the sisters do. She has no private room and her bed is an old army cot. They own no more than a change of clothes and a bucket. They sit on hard benches and eat simple fare.

Her Missionaries of Charity are now operating in sixty-seven countries caring for "the poorest of the poor." The lepers, the retarded, the destitute and the dying, are embraced in the loving arms of this gentle nun. They are not just people to her. They are individuals. She said on *Man Alive* in the late 1960's, "I take one person at a time. We may have 45,000 lepers but I only meet them one at a time. Crippled children, unwanted children, each one is a life to me. I can attend that one person. I can give my whole heart to that one person. I can love that one person for that one time."

It was in 1952 that Mother Teresa opened her home for the dying near the Temple of Kali, the Hindu Goddess of death. She calls it *Nirmal Hriday*, which means Pure Heart. Today, it is one of thirty-two havens for the dying, run by her order, throughout the world.

She told us, "It is awful to be dying and to feel you are a no-body, to feel you are no better than an animal in the street. I remember once picking up a man and bringing him into our home. He said 'Thank God I will die like a human being.' At least as we loved and cared for him we were able to make his last few hours beautiful for him."

She told us that in her view not all poverty was to be found in the slums, not all the hunger experienced by the poor. "There is a poverty of the spirit, a hunger in the soul. A plate of rice or a loaf of bread isn't everything. Too often we allow our means and material things to master us. They break into our lives and cause hunger in our souls. In North America the whole environment is telling us to open up our hearts to Cadillacs, to big houses, to colour television sets. Still, with all this, comes a hunger for spiritual things; a hunger only satisfied by the love of God and the love for our brothers."

The conversation turned to miracles. Did she believe in them?

"Our own lives are miracles aren't they? The fact that we are alive here is a miracle. In my work there is a divine providence. We have no regular income and yet we are able to feed and care for many thousands of people."

There is a story which Malcolm Muggeridge tells in his book *Something Beautiful for God* which suggests that miracles occur in Mother Teresa's presence. He and a British Broadcasting Corporation television crew were filming a documentary about Mother Teresa on location in Calcutta. They wanted to film part of it in her Home For The Dying. It is a large, dark, barn-like building. The only natural light comes from small windows high up on the wall and the technical crew had only one light to illuminate this vast interior. The illumination in what might be considered a well lit room under normal circumstances is usually inadequate for filming. In order for a scene to most resemble what you see with your eye, the intensity of the light must be greatly increased. Muggeridge explains that there was no time to obtain extra lights and against the judgement of the cameraman he decided to proceed. As insurance, however, extra footage was shot in the adjoining courtyard where some inmates had been moved out into the sunshine. In his book, Muggeridge says, "In the processed film the part taken inside was bathed in a particularly beautiful soft light, whereas the part taken outside was dim and confused."

The cameraman, Ken Macmillan, is considered an artist in his profession. He filmed the much acclaimed Kenneth Clark series "Civilization" and his reaction to the Home For The Dying incident was that it was "technically impossible."

Muggeridge bluntly calls it an "actual miracle." He says he is absolutely convinced that the technically unaccountable light came from the love that overflowed the Home For The Dying. He likens it to the light artists have fashioned into halos around the heads of saints and finds it not surprising at all that it should register on photographic film.

I asked Mother Teresa if she thought the mysterious light described by Muggeridge was a miracle.

"Well, it was obviously a miracle for him," she said. "He must have needed one for some reason. Even during the day that place is dark and yet this thing happened around five. Why it happened I don't know. He saw fit to express his feelings about it as a miracle."

In 1976 Mother Teresa came to Toronto and addressed an adoring, overflow crowd at Convocation Hall. She agreed to spend some time with me prior to her appearance. In a secluded corner of the University campus, in the early hours of an April evening, we talked about her work.

"Our purpose," she said, "is to do works of love with people, whether they are Hindu, Moslem or Christian. To be in contact with the poor is a work of love. Any work of love brings a person face to face with God. When this happens hearts are converted and so a Hindu becomes a better Hindu, a Christian becomes a better Christian, a Moslem becomes a better Moslem, a Buddhist becomes a better Buddhist. In this way acts of love and compassion are being relived by everyone. It is putting the love of God into action, into the service of your neighbour. Jesus so often said, 'Love as I have loved you.' He proved his love for us, this is our chance to prove our love for others.''

That statement has always impressed me as the essence of Mother Teresa's philosophy, a conversion of hearts, not of minds, mutual benefit to the giver and the receiver, being a conduit through which love flows to others.

She said, ''The world is suffering much because of a terrible disease. Not leprosy, not tuberculosis, not even hunger, but from not being loved or wanted. It is necessary to feel you are somebody to somebody.''

Mother Teresa told of a recent incident in Calcutta when she and her sisters picked up four people from the streets and took them into *Nirmal Hriday*. One was a woman in very bad condition who Mother Teresa decided to look after herself. She washed her as best she could and put her in a bed.

''She took my hand, and then with such a beautiful smile on her face she said, 'thank you' and she died. I reflected what I would have said if I were she. My sincere answer to myself was that I would likely have tried to draw attention to myself 'I am dying. I am dying. I am in pain. Help me!' Yet this wonderful person said only 'thank you.' She gave me so much more than I had given her.''

She told of a Hindu who had visited her home for the dying and watched a sister washing a person whose open sores were crawling with maggots. Upon leaving he told Mother Teresa, ''I came to this house empty, full of bitterness, but I go out full of God. I have seen the living love of God in action through the hands and through the smile of the sister attending that dying person.''

Mother Teresa speaks in a soft whispery voice. Her words are measured and sparse, with her Yugoslavian accent still evident. Yet in a packed auditorium not a nuance is missed. Her audiences are hushed, held captive by this small serene presence. During her speech she put the philosophy her order exemplifies in the streets of Calcutta into the context of urban life in Toronto. ''Maybe in your own home there are hungry ones, maybe your father or mother, your husband or wife or children, hungry for love, feeling unwanted. Pray that we all may be able to do God's will. What we are doing in the slums, you may not be able to do. On the level that you are called, in your family life, in your college life, in your work life, we cannot do. But we can complete each other, so that you and we together, we are doing something beautiful for God.''

It is difficult to expand on the life of Mother Teresa. It begins and ends with her work in Calcutta and in her relationship with God. All adjectives seem insufficient. Her days are spent in an endless effort to reach as many people as possible. Their lives are her life. They act as doctors, nurses, guardians, but most of all, friends. She is both generous and intelligent, brave and demanding, at home in any setting.

While in Turin, Italy filming a programme on the Shroud, I had occasion to meet Mother Teresa again very briefly. I mention this incident only to show what a delightfully enigmatic woman she is.

Earlier in the day my producer was told that Mother Teresa would be secretly brought into Turin that evening for a brief, private viewing of the Shroud after the Cathedral had been closed for the night and the crowds dispersed.

The possibility of getting her opinion on the Shroud's authenticity outweighed our respect for her request that no media be present.

Accompanied by a veteran *Time* magazine reporter, who was also alerted, we set our camera and lights up on a dark stone balcony direcectly in front of the door, from which Mother Teresa would have to emerge. It was a gamble. Her escorts might simply whisk her by us, but we were the only members of the press, out of the thousands from all over the world who knew about her being in Turin and the smell of a scoop was too strong to ignore.

Finally the heavy doors swung open and a circle of guards, escorts, and police almost hid the tiny grey nun. The *Time* reporter was a real pro. I learned later he had covered Lindbergh's arrival at Orly airfield in Paris, in 1927. He got to her a split second before me and started firing questions.

Mother Teresa paused, looked up into the glare of the television lights and saw me. Her eyes are large, deep and dark. Sometimes they seem so sad and full of anguish they break your heart. This time they were bright and dancing. A smile of recognition spread over her face and she said, "Hello — how are you? I remember you from Toronto. What are you doing here so far away?"

Forgetting I was the one who was supposed to be asking the questions I answered, "We're doing a programme on the Shroud of Turin for *Man Alive*."

"Isn't that wonderful," she said. "How nice to see you again. God bless you!"

With that she simply strode away out of the circle of light and down the cathedral stairs.

She had turned the tables very nicely. I had seen few politicians do it as well. "I didn't ask her what she thought of the Shroud!" I said.

"Shrewd lady," said my producer.

"I'm getting too old for this kind of thing," said the man from *Time*.

You never forget meeting Mother Teresa. You never quite get over it. As with the dying leper in the streets of Calcutta a certain healing takes place. You are better for the meeting. And the only appropriate response from the dying, or the living, is "thank you."

Viktor Frankl

THE CRY
FOR MEANING

*To turn your predicament into an
achievement is to reach the peak of your
capabilities as a human.*

In the spring of 1978, after I had finished speaking at a teachers'
convention in Calgary, a dapper fellow in his forties approached
and said he had arranged with the convention organizer to drive
me to the airport. He had a story he thought I'd like to hear.

The year before had seen him ready to throw in the towel on a
life that, for him, was no longer worth the struggle. Alcoholism
had cost him his job and home. Drugs added to the downward
spiral and his wife and children could take no more. Alone and
sick in a rented room he watched television through a blurry,
alcoholic haze. He said he was literally on the floor watching
when *Man Alive* came on. Being interviewed was Viktor Frankl.
My friend said he didn't know at the time who Frankl was, but
it didn't matter. It was what he said that made the difference.

"He talked about meaning in life, the purpose of being alive,
things that I thought had all gone. I couldn't see any meaning in

my life. I had destroyed all that. Then what he was saying started to make sense. I did a lot of crying and soul-searching that night and decided to start again. I joined Alcoholics Anonymous and stopped doing drugs. It hasn't been easy, but I'm back on my feet now. My former employer took me back and so, thank God, did my wife and family. When I heard that the programme was going to be repeated, I transferred the sound off the TV onto a cartridge tape.'' With that he pushed a button on the dashboard of his car and Frankl's voice echoed through the speakers.

"I know the whole interview by heart now. Every word. I can't tell you how it sustains me and what it has meant in my life!''

We said our goodbyes at the airport. On the plane carrying me back to Toronto I thought back to my conversation with the man who had helped so many awaken to the "meaning" in their lives.

I interviewed Viktor Frankl prior to his appearance at a Massey Hall fund raising event. He had been brought to Toronto by the Youth Corps of the Roman Catholic Church. Its Director, Father Tom McKillop, explained that Frankl had agreed to come on four conditions: he wanted to be advertised and introduced as a Jewish psychiatrist; he would give only one talk to a mass audience open to everyone, (he would return later for a longer period if asked by the psychiatrists professionally); he wanted to talk on the theme "Youth in Search of Meaning"; and he wanted his honorarium to be sent to help the work of Mother Teresa in India.

Frankl is a short, stocky man, with wiry gray hair and thick spectacles. His movements are quick and vibrant and radiate abundant energy. He is seventy-four years old and last year began taking flying lessons in California. His first article was published in 1924 in the *International Journal of Psychoanalysis* at the invitation of Sigmund Freud.

When I spoke with him he was Professor of Neurology and Psychiatry at the University of Vienna Medical School and Professor of Logotherapy at the United States International University in San Diego. He is the originator of what has come to be called the third Viennese school of psychotherapy; the first being Freud's "psychoanalysis" and the second Adler's "individual psychology." Frankl's is "logotherapy."

Frankl is a survivor of four World War II concentration camps. He strongly believes the lesson to be learned from this experience was the same at Auschwitz as in the Japanese prisoner of war camps and later in North Korean and Vietnamese camps. Those prisoners who were oriented toward a meaning to be fulfilled in the future, a task to be done, a person to be met again, were decisively strengthened. They were the most likely to survive. The question was not just survival, there had to be a "why" of survival.

Frankl's theory of logotherapy was born in the concentration camps. Time after time, he observed that unless there was something or someone for whose sake survival was necessary, survival was scarcely possible.

"Can you imagine," he asked me "a situation for a human being which is more full of stress than Auschwitz? But virtually all neurotic symptomology disappeared there. The degree to which suicide took place in Auschwitz and Dachau was surprisingly, astonishingly low. On the other hand a teacher recently showed me a list of questions his pupils wanted to ask him, written up without giving their names, completely anonymous. The spectrum of questions ranged from life on other planets, to drug addiction, sexual problems and so on. Do you know what was the top ranking question, as to frequency, on the list? Suicide! These are youngsters fourteen and fifteen years of age."

"You see," he continued, "we are living in a society, your 'affluent' society here and my 'welfare state' society in Austria, that is out to satisfy and gratify. It looks after every human need but one. And that is the most basic and fundamental need operating in man, the need for meaning. Consumer societies are busy creating needs, but the need for meaning remains unfulfilled. It's what I refer to as the 'unheard cry for meaning.' The basic concern of man is not pleasure or happiness or power or prestige, but to find and fulfill a meaning in each single life situation confronting him. If there is a meaning to fulfill and he is cognizant of it, then he is ready to suffer. He will sacrifice, undergo tension and stress, without any harm being done to his health. But, if there is no meaning available, and none within his visual field, then he takes his life."

My conversation with Viktor Frankl had only just begun, but I was convinced that he was sincere. He had spent a great deal of time analyzing the human condition and would likely spend the rest of his life trying to instill his insights and obvious peace of mind in others. He wasn't just jumping on a bandwagon and cashing in on the popularity of quasi-psychological self-help books. He was not offering pat answers or platitudes designed as a salve rather than a cure. Frankl was drawing on a lifetime of experience, culminating in a well integrated assessment of the importance of meaning in life.

I suggested to Frankl that we were placing too few demands on people today, particularly the young, and that traditional institutions, where we once found meaning, such as the church and family, seemed to have diminished and have taken a less prominent place in our lives.

"You are right in several respects. Thirty years ago I predicted the condition we see emerging today that I call 'the existential vacuum,' a feeling of emptiness, a sense of futility. This takes over from the inferiority feelings and the sexual frustrations we are aware of from Freud.

"This mass neurosis of meaninglessness can be explained in two ways. First, in contrast to animals, man is not told by driving instincts what he 'must' do. Second, in contrast to man in former times, he is no longer told by traditions and universally-held values what he 'should' do. Sometimes he no longer seems to know what he basically wishes to do. The consequence is this, either he just does what other people are doing, this is conformism, or, he just does what other people wish him to do, and this is totalitarianism. This is the origin of the "existential vacuum.' "

It was apparent to me that the people who are most affected by this loss of traditional values are the young. I asked Frankl how this situation should be remedied.

"Young people today have virtually no stress or tension because they are pampered," he answered. "We do not challenge them. What young people need are ideals, challenges, personal tasks, but most of all, examples. They don't need examples from cowards, people who are afraid to confront them with anything because it might make them angry. Neither the parents nor the school teachers seem courageous enough to challenge them for fear of arousing tensions. Young people today are not overdemanded."

We talked for a while about the place of religion in one's life, whether faith in God helped one discover meaning. "Let's say I'm just an average sort of chap. I have never been tested by suffering. I live a very comfortable life and don't feel a need to believe in God, perhaps I'm bored with my job, and my family. Now you say I can still find meaning in life. Where? How?"

Frankl replied, "I would concede personally that it is easier to find meaning in life if you are a religious person. But, on the other hand, you cannot command a person to believe. Faith must grow within yourself, organically. But meaning can be found by each and every person irrespective of his age, sex, educational background, I.Q., personal character structure, or psychological makeup, even irrespective of environment. Think again of Auschwitz. Irrespective of whether or not he is religious and, if he is religious, to what denomination he belongs.

"There are three main avenues leading to meaning, fulfillment. The first is through work, creating work or doing a deed. The second is through love, through experiencing someone in his very uniqueness and this means loving. Work and love are the main paths leading up to meaning. But, you can find the deepest possible meaning through adversity. If you are confronted with a fate you no longer can change, say an incurable disease, you may find the highest conceivable meaning. Then you have the opportunity to bear witness to human potential at its best, which is to turn a tragedy into a personal triumph. To turn your predicament into an achievement is to reach the peak of your capabilities as a human."

Dr. Frankl stressed that suffering was not an end unto itself. To endure unnecessary suffering did not yield meaning. I asked him if it was necessary sometimes to hit bottom before one discovered meaning in life.

"I get many letters from people in prisons. Some have said that only there, in their cells, a few hundred feet from the electric chair, have they discovered meaning. The problem is our view of ourselves. If we are indoctrinated with the view that man is nothing but a mechanism, nothing more than the outcome of conditioning or psychodynamic processes, small wonder we purge from him any enthusiasm or idealism."

I suggested that some people put little value on this life because they expect something better in an afterlife. Life is transitory and our belief in a better life after death keeps us from living fully, here and now. As a medical doctor he must have experienced this many times; the patient who questioned making the effort to live, since death was inevitable.

"Only potentialities are transitory," he answered. "The opportunities to fulfill meaning, to do something, to be loved by someone, to shoulder something courageously, even facing your death in a dignified manner, these are opportunities for us and we should use them. Then our past becomes important. When all this meaning is safely delivered and deposited in the past, nobody can rob us of it. A deed done, a love loved, a suffering honestly gotten through, these are indelible. When we look back on our life we usually just see the stubble field in the past. We overlook the full granaries into which we have rescued and deposited our deeds, our experiences, our sufferings; the harvest of our lives.

"The past is the safest form of being. It is over, but everything remains. We have eternalized everything. Rather than looking for a future, or an afterlife we need a sense of personal responsibility; the feeling that I'm responsible for what I'm putting into the past and nobody can undo what I have done."

I was curious about Frankl's views on society's current preoccupation with materialism and self indulgence, the emphasis on looking out for number one, self fulfillment and personal gratification.

"Forgive my contradicting the American Declaration of Independence," he said, "but I deem the 'pursuit of happiness' a contradiction in terms. Happiness can never really be pursued. Happiness must ensue. It is a side effect, a by-product of your dedication to a task or a cause greater than yourself.

"This is very conspicuous in sexual neurosis. A person who hunts, chases or pursues sexual happiness or pleasure is doomed to failure. A male patient who is bent on demonstrating his sexual potency winds up with impotence. A female patient, to the degree she pursues her own orgasm ability, often becomes frigid. On the other hand, the more you give of yourself, the more you forget yourself, in love or in work, for the sake of a cause to serve, or a person to love, to that very extent you will become happy precisely by not caring for happiness."

He told me of an experience in Melbourne, Australia where he was giving a lecture at the university. Following his speech he was presented with a boomerang for a souvenir. He, like many others, assumed that the purpose of the boomerang's unique design was so it would return to the hunter or thrower. His Australian friends explained that if it did return it meant that the target had been missed. He said he suddenly had an insight that the boomerang was the very symbol of human existence, that those people who keep returning to themselves, who had not connected with people other than themselves, had missed, not a target so much as a mission in life. "Not being primarily concerned with oneself, but something other, or still better someone other than oneself, is to be fully human."

During the interview I noticed a man in a wheelchair who was listening intently from a corner of the studio. Since extra people are often around during a taping I paid little attention to him until after the interview was over.

Father Tom McKillup, who had brought Dr. Frankl to the studio, wheeled the man up and said, "I'd like you to meet John Howard Griffith."

The name rang a bell immediately, though I hadn't heard of

the man for many years. Back in the 1950's I had followed, along with millions of others, Griffith's incredible story of racial bigotry in *Black Like Me*.

A white newspaper reporter, Griffith had dyed his skin in order to penetrate the world of the American black. The result was a book of such revealing insight that white consciences were shocked with an intensity unfelt since *Uncle Tom's Cabin*.

Now ill and crippled by a malignancy caused by the poisonous dye, Griffith had journeyed from his home in Texas to hear Frankl speak in Toronto. His life, too, had been touched by this vigorous intellect that espoused meaning as the central reason for living.

I reflected that Griffith's life was exactly what Frankl had been talking about; life with a purpose, with work, with caring for a cause or someone other than yourself, and with the kind of suffering that "bears witness to the human potential."

Elizabeth Kubler-Ross

WHAT HAPPENS
WHEN YOU DIE?

*The last thing on my mind was life
after death. I am as surprised as anyone
else to find it is true.*

A few years ago a United Church minister approached me after
a meeting in Vancouver and said he had a story in which I might
be interested.

The previous spring he had suffered a heart attack and for
several hours was in a very deep coma. A hastily summoned doctor actually pronounced him dead when to the surprise of everyone he "awoke" and told them of his experience.

He had been working in his office at home a month earlier
when a sharp pain stabbed his chest. He remembers slumping
over his desk and trying to call for help. Suddenly he could see
the entire scene from some point above the desk, near the ceiling
of the room. He watched the door open and his wife rush in and
frantically call the doctor. His teenage children helped his wife
lift his body onto the office couch, unbutton his collar, remove
his shoes and cover him with a blanket. This was the last he saw

of the room. He became aware of a strong yellow light pulling him down a "tunnel-like passage." It was a pleasant feeling. He experienced no fear, only curiosity. He reasoned that this must be death, in which case, it didn't seem too bad at all. He had no indication of time or place, but near the end of the tunnel he felt he was coming to a point of no return. He thought of his wife and family and things that he had not done. He was conscious of weighing on one hand the attractive possibility of continuing on out of the tunnel into what appeared to be a dazzling white light or being pulled back to look after unfinished business.

"I realized that I was being given a glimpse of what death was. There was no need to fear. I figured it would always be thus. There were some pressing personal matters that needed me now more than death did. I found myself returning somewhat reluctantly back through the tunnel and into my body. The soreness of my chest and an aching head told me I was once again ' alive.' "

This was not the first time I had heard of such an experience, but it was the first related to me personally by someone I knew and trusted. One of the most celebrated cases is that of Dr. Carl Jung, the noted psychiatrist and colleague of Sigmund Freud. Jung also had a heart attack. He described his brief clinical "death." "It seemed to me I was high up in space," he wrote, "far below I saw a globe of earth bathed in glorious blue light. Ahead of me I saw a shining temple and was drawn toward it.... I had the certainty I was about to enter an illuminated room and meet there all those people who I loved in reality. There I would at last understand the meaning of life." At this point Jung's doctor injected a heart stimulant and Jung was "regretfully pulled back" into his body. He found this world drab in comparison to what he had been privileged to glimpse.

Because of his reputation Jung's story carried a great deal of weight. Many other stories of out-of-body experiences at the time of death emerged over the years, but were treated for the most part as frauds or delusions. It wasn't until another internationally known figure affirmed these and other stories that the topic again received such wide attention. Dr. Elizabeth Kubler-Ross is a noted psychiatrist whose studies of the dying have been highly acclaimed all over the world. She gave credence to the movement by declaring in 1975, "My talks with hundreds of people who have been resuscitated convince me beyond a shadow of a doubt that there is life after death."

She described three components common to these death experiences, a sense of the soul floating out of the body, a feeling of peace and wholeness, and a meeting with someone who had previously died.

Dr. Kubler-Ross' high standing among health professionals and the general public helped focus immediate attention on her findings. It also raised theological questions. Is the transition from life to an afterlife to be understood as an extension of natural life or does it depend on a special divine hand?

Most religious thinkers I have discussed this with seem pleased that scientists are studying the subject and see Dr. Kubler-Ross' disclosures as confirmation of their belief in eternal life.

Dr. Raymond A. Moody Jr., a resident in psychiatry, hit the best seller lists with his book *Life After Life* which detailed some fifty case studies that revealed patterns almost identical to those found by Dr. Kubler-Ross in her recent investigations.

In her foreword to his book, Dr. Kubler-Ross wrote that the account was true because "it was written by a genuine and honest investigator. It is also corroborated by my own research and by the findings of other(s)" investigating this field for "those who need to know rather than to believe." This assessment seemed so unscientific, even to my ears, I was anxious to find out if controlled scientific proof would emerge or whether Kubler-Ross' findings were to be accepted on trust alone.

I talked with both Dr. Moody and Dr. Kubler-Ross in separate interviews to explore the subject further and to let our audience hear their amazing stories.

Dr. Moody does not claim scientific proof of an afterlife. He told me, "I'm aware that I'm a very fallible human being. I realize that what I've done is an anecdotal kind of study that does not constitute evidence in a scientific sense. I will say that after talking with hundreds of people who have been through these encounters with death, I accept the fact they went through something real. I don't say that as Raymond Moody, philosophy professor, or Raymond Moody, physician, but just as me. That has been my own psychological response to this kind of thing."

Dr. Moody has interviewed over four hundred people. I was curious to discover if he agreed with Dr. Kubler-Ross, and thought there were common denominators involved. If so, what were they?

"People report that at the time of their close approach to death they hear troubling auditory sensations, a buzzing or roaring. Then they feel they're drawn very rapidly through a darkened enclosure, often called a tunnel, a pipe, or a cave. At the end of this they may be quite surprised to find themselves looking on their own physical bodies from a point of view outside themselves. People have described to me how they were just below the ceiling of the emergency room in a hospital watching themselves being operated on. Many also say that relatives and friends who'd already died were there in some form to help them through this transition. They have also talked about, what is called 'panoramic memory' in which every single thing they had ever done was portrayed there. It's all around them in full colour, three dimensional and very often from a third person point of view, that is, they were seeing themselves from a distance doing these things.''

She is no stranger to Canada having been involved in many consultations and lecture tours in this country. She had been included in an earlier *Man Alive* programme about palliative care. The CBC also produced a widely distributed film *To Die Today* featuring Dr. Kubler-Ross. She is on the advisory board of the Canadian Institute of Psychosynthesis and the city of Regina, Saskatchewan made her an honorary citizen.

It was because of her tremendous reputation that I pressed harder than usual for concrete facts. A scientist of her stature exerts a considerable amount of influence and therefore has a responsibility to back up any claim of factual evidence.

"My interest was never to find out whether there was life after death. I was the classical wishy-washy Protestant and even when I started working with dying patients and they would ask me if there was life after death, I would say 'I'm the wrong person to ask, I probably have more questions than you have.' When you are a general practitioner you refer people with specific problems to a specialist. So, I would refer these patients to a clergyman. Unfortunately, the clergy didn't know either. Some, of course, do believe, but my studies show that forty-nine per cent of the clergy do not believe in life after death. These clergymen just give the patients nice phrases and comfortable words instead of telling them the truth, which I do now.

"It is terribly important for people to realize what is relevant in life. If you could teach your children that God is unconditional love and not a judgmental, punitive, discriminating kind of a monster, millions of people would be different.

"If you can tell parents whose child has been brutally raped, murdered and dumped in a pond, and I know horrible cases of this, that at the moment of death the human being has the ability to shed the physical body like a butterfly from its cocoon, that there is no agony, no pain, no fear, think what this means for parents who relive a horrible crime, maybe for years, and who go nearly insane wondering about the aloneness and agony of their child's death.''

I told Dr. Kubler-Ross I didn't want to know what was going to happen in the future. I thought it was better to live just one day at a time. I found the whole mystery of life and death very important. If the mystery was removed some of the quality of this life would go with it.

She didn't agree. ''Knowing about life after death enhances the quality of this life a thousand-fold. The biggest problem with the majority of my dying patients is when they look back and say 'I made a good living. I built a beautiful home. I sent my children to a terrific college. I really worked hard and was a good provider.' There is a real sadness when they tell me this, because they never took time out to get to know these children. When they get another chance, they go home and draw up different plans. They take their son fishing, spend more time with the family. They learn that all your mansions on earth, all your degrees and honours, are irrelevant.''

''The description of this 'unobstructed universe' is based on people who have not really died, but, have had a near death experience then been resuscitated and have told us about it,'' I commented. This conversation followed.

''That is part of it.''

''But we have no concrete evidence?''

''It has not been published.''

''Oh, then there is more evidence to back this up?''

''Oh yeah!''

''When am I going to see this?''

''Probably within the next year.''

''You are publishing this?''

''Yes.''

''Could you let me have a little bit of it now, just an example? I can't just go on people's stories. If I had something more specific.''

''What about it bothers you, that you won't go on people's stories.''

''Because these people haven't really died. It could be some mental activity.''

''O.K. Let's discuss that.''

''Alright. Perhaps the heart has stopped beating, but the brain is still alive. It could be residual mental activity that accounts for the images they are getting. An out-of-the-body experience may not even be happening.''

"You can teach people clinically, scientifically and in a laboratory to have an out-of-the-body experience."

"Have you had one?"

"I have had them in a laboratory, hooked up to polygraphs. You can on command, at your wish, on your deciding, leave your body."

At this point Dr. Kubler-Ross pointed to the ceiling of the television studio, high above the lights.

"I would ask you how many layers of material are in your roof, how much insulation. You can have an out-of-body experience then come back and tell me the answer. I can wish to be with my friends in San Francisco and by having an out-of-body experience I can tell you what they have on their kitchen table. Now you tell me how you explain that. I have done it in a laboratory to verify it. There is a great deal of research going on in this field and believe me, I would not ruin my professional reputation and say things unless I were one hundred per cent sure."

When I asked about the benefit of this research she told of a Vietnam veteran, a parapelegic, who was confined to a wheel chair in a veterans' hospital. His out-of-body experiences allowed him to attend football games. His physical body remained in the hospital, but he could attend the games and didn't even need to buy a ticket.

Certainly, many people who have had close brushes with death find life more precious and behave in a different manner, but I wanted her to describe the beyond for me. What kind of place was it? Was it Heaven? She didn't want me to call it a "place." She preferred the terminology "unobstructed universe."

"The first thing to know is that you are with your loved ones. You can never die alone."

I asked her what these people looked like, and how would we know them.

"Only shortly after death will they appear in their physical bodies to give you a chance to recognize them. You obviously know your child or your mother or father."

"But I'm wondering how they look," I continued, "a lot of people on their death bed don't look very good."

"They look young and healthy," she explained. "They look the way they feel would appeal to you the most. If you had a marvelous time with your mother when she was fifty, that's how she would come to you, the way she looked when you had the best time together. It is their choice, they can appear any way that is the most appealing to you. But, afterwards they don't need that

143

anymore. All human beings after this just become energy patterns."

"Could you meet historic figures then?" I asked.

"Oh yes," she answered, "you could meet anyone you loved and admired. You also have all the music you want."

"What kind of music?"

"You tune in to any wave length you like. If you like Hank Williams, or Beethoven you could select them. In this room right now is the music of Mozart. You don't hear him and I don't hear him, but if we tuned the radio to the right frequency we'd hear Mozart. You don't hear the sound a dog whistle makes but the dog does. It's all a question of energy."

"Speaking of dogs, are there animals there too?"

"Only at the time of the transition. If a woman for example has been really attached to her poodle, perhaps she had no children, this poodle will come to her at the beginning. The only animals we have heard of are cats and dogs."

I asked her if we all went to the same "place" regardless of how we had behaved on this earth. She claimed we did and that there would be no problem with over-crowding since there was no sense of time or space. It did, however, make a difference how we had lived since we would be required to evaluate every single aspect of our entire existence. This would be done in the presence of an "unconditional love." Some people call it Christ, some call it God, some call it "the light" but most people call it love. The transition to this unobstructed universe is the same for a Hitler as a Mother Teresa. You are asked in the presence of this unconditional love to look at your deeds, your fruits, your words and you will be given all knowledge to recall them. You will also know instantaneously how every one of your actions and thoughts have affected others and that is, symbolically speaking, going through hell.

Stories related to life after death experiences and out-of-body travels tend to fall in the same category as UFO sightings. We take them with a grain of salt until they are recounted by someone we respect and trust. Certainly Dr. Elizabeth Kubler-Ross, with her scientific background and her world-wide reputation, would be, to many, a credible witness. I asked her if she realized the responsibility she bore to millions of people in making these statements. There was a long pause. For a while I thought she wasn't going to answer. Then she said, "Yes, I know that. I don't think you are aware of the pain it causes me. It is very difficult when my husband gets letters saying that I am psychotic and need

144

phychiatric help before it's too late! These letters are often signed 'In Christ, a friend.' They don't have the courage to sign their own names. Do you know what this does to a family? Besides that, you get homicidal threats, 'If life after death is so beautiful, we'll be glad to come over and help you out.' And people who used to be your friends get frightened and one after the other they fall away. I'm not taking it lightly. To me it's very important. I believe it and I've always followed through on what I believe. My book on dying patients was a great preparation for this, because there was a lot of hostility about it, but it was worthwhile.''

I assured her that I wasn't suggesting she didn't believe in what she was saying, quite obviously she did. ''But isn't there a chance that you have worked with dying patients for so long, seen such great suffering, tried to help so many, that you want very much to believe there is something more for them?''

''I have evaluated my motives for a long time. I never planned what I am doing. The last thing on my mind was life after death. I am as surprised as anyone else to find it is true. I could really exist without that belief because I feel I have had a super life. I have really lived. I've put a lot into life and gotten a lot out of it. If I had been raised, say, a Baptist with a very fundamentalist Christian background, I might want to prove that this is true like some fanatic. My childhood was in the most liberal, semi-religious environment you could imagine. I am one of triplets. One married a Catholic, one a Jew and one a Protestant. So I have no hangups.''

During the interview Dr. Kubler-Ross told me about *Shanti-Nilaya*, a forty-two acre ranch northeast of San Diego, which she and her husband purchased in 1976 for $262,500. At this time she formed a partnership with Jay Barham a former Arkansas farmer, San Diego airplane factory worker and founder of the Church of the Facet of Divinity, a year old gathering of about two hundred followers in the Escondido area of California. She became very impressed with what she called Barham's ''healing powers'' and his ''ability to communicate with the spirits.''

Shanti Nilaya, which is Sanskrit for ''Home of Peace'' is advertised as a non-profit organization holding seminars and workshops for the terminally ill and the bereaved. Clients pay only enough for room and board and receive therapy and attend counselling sessions. The staff also investigates psychic healing and administers ''life, death and transition'' workshops involving psycho drama and techniques that are supposed to help people relieve themselves of guilt.

In the fall of 1979 it was revealed that state and local authorities were investigating charges that participants in some of the sessions had been injured and that Barham had sexually molested several women and a child while posing as a spirit. Three former female members of Barham's church claimed that during séances he would instruct them to enter a side room where a naked man would join them a few minutes later claiming to be an "afterlife entity." This entity would then proceed to have sex with them. There was never any hint that Dr. Kubler-Ross was directly involved, but because of her association with Barham and her high profile, she was "tarred with the same brush."

The scandal stunned the Kubler-Ross faithful. This was the final assault on a distinguished and gentle woman. Then her husband of twenty years, neurologist Emmanuel Ross, divorced her. He retained their family home in Chicago, a beautiful structure designed by Frank Lloyd Wright.

The complaints of the three women were never proved. The San Diego District Attorney's office investigated the reports, including one that a ten year old girl was molested, but dropped the case for lack of evidence.

Dr. Kubler-Ross fought back. On national television she defended herself and Jay Barham. "My workshops have young dying children and grandmothers in their nineties," she exclaimed, "with the dignity and beauty of these people do you think there's any place for orgies?"

With her husband, home and most of her close friends gone Dr. Kubler-Ross maintains a hectic pace. She travels about two hundred and fifty thousand miles per year and accepts only one in every thirty speaking invitations. Her $3,000 speaking fee is donated to *Shanti Nilaya* which has now set up branches in Rhode Island, Hawaii, New Jersey and Australia. Claiming success in psychic treatment of victims of epilepsy and severe emotional problems she pays tribute to Barham. "He has done more healing in the last six months than in my wildest dreams. If people would only get in touch with their spirits, they would be able to heal, emotionally and physically."

Her new book did not contain the scientific evidence which she promised would prove her afterlife claims. Many more of her friends and colleagues in the scientific community lost patience and faith in their former heroine. This does not dampen her enthusiasm or alter her beliefs. She says, "there is no doubt that death is simply a shedding of the physical body and a transition to a higher state of consciousness. When I see people at the

146

moment of their death it is as if they have just dropped their old shabby winter coat which they don't need anymore because spring is coming.''

Given her qualifications and her obvious sincerity it is difficult not to believe this remarkable woman when sitting across from her listening to her calm and matter of fact statements, and perhaps I should. But I keep wondering if it really matters at all. Could it be that life is meant to be lived fully without any knowledge of what happens after it ends? To live each day as it comes, being as completely and fully human as we can; using whatever abilities and intelligence we have developed, without concern for whatever lies beyond, seems to me a good way to spend our time here on earth. I'm willing to let the mystery of afterlife remain exactly that. At least I won't have wasted precious moments of this life worrying about it.

"What has been described in many of these cases as 'a being of light' manifests itself. Christians identify this as being Christ; Jews will call it the supreme being or use another word, but the descriptions are very much the same. They feel that this being asks them questions. 'What have you done with your life that you want to show me?', is a very common formulation. The point of the question they feel, is to make them face it. It is translated by these people as meaning not how much money did you have, or how much power did you have, or what clubs did you belong to, but in the course of your life have you been able to love your fellow human beings? This can make a powerful emotional impact on people, especially when they return to life. They realize they should be living in certain ways. They also understand that death is not to be feared. It is not an obliteration. It is, rather, transitional. Many say they do want to come back because they have some specific thing in life they want to complete. The most common is that they want to continue raising their children or some other family matter.''

Raymond Moody told me that in his opinion these near death experiences could not be dismissed as delusions induced by painkilling drugs or any of the other sceptical, pat answers. The stories he says are too clear and too similar to each other not to be trusted.

While Moody would not claim that his investigations should be regarded as proof, I sensed he personally had little doubt about the existence of life after death. I asked him if the publicity had changed Raymond Moody. He answered laughingly, ''My wife and I realized recently that half of our friends have 'been

147

dead.' We've gotten to know these people very well. We have established a close personal relationship with them. I think a lot of what they've been through has rubbed off on me. My personal response is that I do not doubt there is survival of bodily death and that makes a great deal of difference, you know. It makes life very precious. I would like to go on living and getting things done here and be able to say after death that I have lived a life for others. I want very much to make that my personal goal.''

Unlike Dr. Moody, Dr. Elizabeth Kubler-Ross is quite prepared to claim scientific proof of life after death. Claiming it and proving it, however, are two different things. My persistence in asking for proof and pushing for hard evidence during our conversation evoked a flood of protest letters from viewers who thought I was attacking this revered scientist. Far from it. I have long respected Dr. Kubler-Ross and greatly admire her significant contribution to the care of the dying.

Dr. Elizabeth Kubler-Ross was born in Zurich, Switzerland in 1926. In 1957 she received her MD from the university there, then moved to the United States for her internship. The list of honours bestowed upon her seems endless. Kubler-Ross has been a consultant to over thirty major clinics, institutes, hospitals and hospices. One hospice in Florida bears her name. Dying was the subject of all her writing, published throughout the world. Her works include an article in the Encyclopedia Britannica and her most famous book, *On Death and Dying*, published in 1969, which is considered a hand book for doctors, nurses, psychiatrists, clergy and lay people all over the world.

Germaine Greer

HUMAN SEXUALITY

*The great thing, of course, would be to
have women so in tune with their bodies that
they actually knew what was going on.*

I didn't know very much about Germaine Greer in 1977 except
that she was a leading feminist and the author of *The Female
Eunuch*, but her articles on women's sexuality in *Esquire, Play-
boy* and *Harper's* made her a good person to interview on the
subject of contraception. She had toured North America speaking out against the pill and suggesting that women stop using
modern contraceptive methods.

My producer planned to get a few statements from her on the
subject to include in a programme tracing the history of contraception and its modern misuse. After filming the interview he decided he had enough information for a separate programme as
well, since Germaine Greer had talked at length about human
sexuality in general.

My image of Germaine Greer was of a tough, pugnacious,
militant woman who didn't particularly care for men and de-

lighted in deflating their egos. Instead, I found a warm, generous person, who spoke with intelligence and wit about what was happening to women and men alike.

Her modest, but comfortable home in the Notting Hill Gate section of London, England has a lived-in, welcoming atmosphere. She wasn't there when we arrived for our early morning filming, but a note pinned to the door told us to make ourselves at home, as she had rushed her cat to the veterinarian for some undetermined illness.

There was some discussion about doing the programme in the bedroom because of the topic under discussion, but she was aware of her image as a sexually liberated woman and thought the kitchen would be better since she did indeed spend a great deal of time there and we could sip coffee while we talked.

She spoke in a straightforward, lucid and dynamic manner that required no prodding on my part. We found later that it was one of the few interviews where little editing was required. Everything was clear, concise, and usable.

We were aware that her unorthodox opinions and her salty descriptive language would probably shock some viewers, but here was an intelligent, caring person speaking out honestly and passionately on an important subject with great expertise. She has made a lifelong study of the history and present condition of the female in our society. Greer feels understanding sexuality is a crucial element in the understanding of women as a whole.

Eyes flashing with indignation, she lashed out at today's scientific methods of contraception.

"The thought of a sixteen year old girl whose uterus isn't fully developed and who doesn't even know what normality would be, because she has no idea what her sexual chemistry is, using massive hormonal preparations on a daily basis, is terrifying to me, especially because there is now emerging a syndrome of sterility in women who began to use the pill at an early age. They are coming off the pill after ten years at twenty-six and they don't get pregnant.

"Take a look at what the pill does to ordinary secretions in the vagina. Normally speaking a healthy vagina is very good at defending itself against trauma. But if you take the pill the chemical balance in the vagina is disturbed. You get the beginning of trivial patterns of infection, just ordinary infections in the skin. Then you get an advancing profile of a galaxy of small infections and finally you get the biggies.

"The story of candidiasis, for example, is absolutely pill generated. Candida used to be a normal vaginal flora that lived there along with everything else. The pill upset the sugar balance in the vagina in such a way that candida became carnivorous, turned into a cannibal mechanism, chomped up all the other flora, created a situation of severe imbalance and began to chomp into the host itself. So you have a painful, purilent infection that is venereal because you can spread it by sexual contact.

"I think a lot of the problems that we have now, especially in North America, but also in Europe, with low grade pelvic inflammation is due to the effects the pill has on the body's natural defences.

"The other thing is that women who take the pill become totally accessible to the male at all times. They have no non-inflammatory reason for saying no. Nowadays women who are pilled up and ready to go have made an investment in sexual action. And it's a pretty hefty investment. No woman takes the pill and thinks that it's just an aspirin.

"Being constantly sterile is an inducement to sexual activity which isn't really worth it. It really wouldn't do you any harm not to have it. You may not even want it all that much. We know that women don't get their principle sexual pleasure from intromission. They enjoy least of all, or with the most difficulty, the kind of sexual intercourse or interplay that leads to pregnancy. What they've done by using all these contraceptives, pills, coils, gadgets, odds and ends, is to make themselves available for intromission, not for sex, but for a specific kind of sex that nowadays people think is co-extensive with the whole of sexual practice, and they call it by silly puritanical names. They call it normal sex. Well, who said it was normal?"

She was equally outspoken on other methods of contraception.

"To tell a young girl to have an IUD or a coil, well, you wouldn't get me to do that at gunpoint. The coil is an abortive agent, not a contraceptive at all. You may actually be becoming pregnant only you don't know it.

"You could meet a woman tomorrow, say you're fifty years old, she wants your baby and you want to give it to her, but there was that vasectomy back when you were forty-five, how ridiculous! Besides which, people usually have vasectomies for the wrong reason. They have vasectomies because in a certain partnership no more children are wanted. Usually it's the woman who says 'that's enough.' The man hasn't thought about it or doesn't really care that much. Now, what hapens if the marriage breaks up? What happens if she falls in love with somebody else? How much loathing and vengefulness must he feel? I've come across it in very young men.

"A lot of abortions that take place are not really wanted by the people who are having them. They are wanted by their parents or the court, or the school teacher, the child's peer group or by the boy-friend. And if the man you love wants you to have an abortion, you have an abortion, even though you don't really want it.

"An abortion is relatively easy since a woman does it all the time anyway. She probably aborts naturally more than she ever brings to full term. Nobody knows how many fetuses are aborted in life because it happens at all stages in the cycle, most of them undetectable.

"If done early enough an abortion is a trivial happening that doesn't even cause discomfort. On the other hand most contraception is a complex, ponderous, chemical effort to render a woman sterile for a pre-determined period.

"Many women today are totally infertile and about one in eight are sub-fertile. What's the point of bombarding her with dangerous chemicals that have cumulative effects because they derail important endocrine processes for long periods? These processes are needed to keep tissues young and growing and replacing themselves. What is the point in doing that if she will never be pregnant? Why not let her find out that she may never be pregnant? Would it be a disaster to let every woman get pregnant once just to see if she can do it? I don't think it would!

"The women in my mother's generation had no scruples about asking men to practice coitus interuptus. That was not an extraordinary demand. I've talked to men about it. They don't really mind doing it. It is a different kind of sexuality which we have been brought up to stigmatize as being totally abnormal. If it were abnormal then entire races of people from Iceland to Bangkok would be stark raving mad. You may consider that they are, I don't know.

"The Italians, for example, still practice coitus interuptus. It's one of the features in their perpetual semi-tumescence, their perpetual state of excitement, their susceptibility to women.

"It is more effective as a birth control method than people think. It's not one hundred per cent effective, but it certainly lowers the birth rate. Peasant families that I know in Italy, for example, have an average of two children per family and when you ask them how they did it, they all give the same answer — coitus interuptus. So it is not one hundred per cent effective.

Neither is the diaphram and neither, my God, is the much vaunted coil!

"Sometimes, I say don't do it. When women say to me 'I've tried the pill. I've tried the coil. I've done this. I've had an ectopic pregnancy with my coil and half my womb fell out. What do I do now?' Well, I say, knock it off for a while. Do something else! Why do you have to keep on doing it? What's so good about it in preference to something else? A lot of women are having sex they don't really want at all. Better to not do it at all, than to keep on doing it badly."

In her 1970 best seller, *The Female Eunuch*, Germaine Greer wrote "security is when everything is settled, when nothing can happen to you. Security is a denial of life." I suggested to her that this sounded as though she wanted women to live more dangerously.

"Not really, I think they already live very dangerously," she answered. "I think they live on the edge of a precipice. What I can't bear is their ignorance and incuriosity based on fear.

"When you ask them what they think of the contraceptive they are using they say 'Oh, it's fine.' They mean, 'It works. I'm not pregnant and don't worry me!' I want them to realize how dangerously they are living. I want them to look their own behaviour in the eye and see what it really means. Work it all out. How much pleasure? How much pain? How much anxiety? How much expense of spirit? It's hard to get them to do that. Women are so beaten down that their courage is at a low ebb. They have to struggle so hard to keep their heads together in whatever situation they find themselves."

During the course of the interview Germaine used the word "intromission" instead of "intercourse." I asked her for her definition of sexual intercourse.

"The term sexual intercourse itself is vague. It is intercourse of a sexual nature, which is conversation and dealings of all sorts. If you go to lunch and sit down with people, you are sexually aware of the people you are with. You are aware of the antagonism of some of the women, or their susceptibility and vulnerability to you. All of that is sexual intercourse and you use that to varying degrees. You can indicate you don't want to entertain it in various ways or you can encourage it. If the occasion is a success there will be a kind of general sexual loosening between the people. This is really sexual, though it's not genital. You don't suddenly leap on the floor and start having an orgy.

"The thing that isn't all that important is the obligatory, suburban intromission period twice a week or seven times a week or whatever. And too often when people ask the question 'what about sex' in the marriage guidance councils, they mean 'what's your intromission count?' Then they go into all that fifties stuff about 'he should last longer' and 'waiting for her' and 'twiddling this and doing that,' and Dr. Rubin and blah, blah, blah....

"That's really not what it's all about. It's about taking joy from each other's bodies no matter which way it goes. And I think in some cases relationships are more stable when the sexual element becomes less important. By its very nature it's unpredictable and sometimes disappointing. It has its own built-in curve of gratification. A relationship that's going to last should be built by a different architect. It has to have different priorities. Some people are lucky enough to go on having intense sexual, genital involvement for fifty years, but I think they must be very few. The ones that really make it are the ones that don't get into a state if, for a few years, they go through a rather dreary patch where other people seem more attractive to them. There is a strange American attitude that doesn't prevail in England, a conviction on the part of women that men who wish to go to bed with them are doing them down in some sort of way. I don't think that feeling prevails in Europe. I'm usually delighted when a man shows that he is sexually susceptible to me. I like that. I don't think 'Oh, you dirty thing!' Then there is, correspondingly, a sort of rage if the man is not duly tumescent and overbearing in his bed manners. There seems to be a sort of challenging, a sort of sporting attitude to it. I think probably in Europe it makes more sense to say that it's 'amorous conversation' between the sexes. We still flirt in Europe you know."

For Germaine Greer there are no ideal man-woman sexual relationships. Whatever is right for you and your partner is what matters. Feelings are all important. Relationships that are comfortable and pleasurable are desirable, instead of trying to live up to what society or moralists expect.

"There are a million different relationships you can have. A relationship between a mother and father is not the same as a relationship between lovers. One reason we get so muddled up is that young people have their babies when they are still madly in love with each other. They don't know what to do with their babies. I would have a different relationship with a man who was actually going to be the father of my child than I would with a man I fell in love with on a weekend in Tunis.

"I'm having a relationship at the moment with a man that I

never expect to make love to and it doesn't worry me at all because it's such an amazing turn-on. I feel so much more loving to the rest of the world because he is in it.

"You see we've made all this fuss and bother about orgasms. We've made a whole culture out of it. It's easy. It's a cinch to have an orgasm. I can give an orgasm to my cat! It's really very trivial. One of these days we'll get orgasms out of the way and we can then get on with the business of actually knowing each other. To draw excitement from a relationship is not a matter of a spasm racking you every twenty-four hours."

"The great thing of course would be to have women so in tune with their bodies that they actually knew what was going on. Our 'body-blindness' is one of the factors in the situation. If we weren't so body-blind we couldn't bear the coil. In areas where women are not so estranged from their bodies, Asia for example, they have much more trouble with the coil. They really can't tolerate it. They give birth to the damn thing. They are just not about to go around with this piece of plumbers equipment dangling in their cervix. They can't tolerate it at all.

"I think the diaphram is so disgusting. No girl who is still finding out what it's like to make love should have to find out with a rubber dingy inside her full of stinking 'blanc-mange.' It puts tremendous limitations on the kind of sex she will have. It puts the emphasis on intromission because that's all you can do. You can't go down on a woman who's got a mercuric spermacide oozing out of her...you'd be crazy or suicidal or something.

"I find it staggering that science hasn't improved the diaphram in fifty years. In fact it has actually deteriorated. The original diaphrams were small. They fitted nicely. They had a small dab of spermicide that went in them. You didn't end up awash with a dreadful, white mess. Now, we have these dreadful huge things that if you can get them in at all, are supposed to somehow fit. The spermicides became much more dangerous and also nastier in terms of what they did to sensation and God knows what the effect of absorbing them through the vaginal mucosa must be over long periods. I don't think anyone has done any work on that at all. I think that's astonishing. You could, it seems to me, have a custom-built diaphram that fitted absolutely neatly, that was disposable, that you didn't have to wash and hang out to dry and all that nonsense.

"It is unbelievable the crude and gross state of medicine in this area. My favourite parallel is between the North American mouth and the North American vagina. The North American mouth is a multi-billion dollar industry with a profit margin of four hundred per cent or something — and the vagina, what does it have? It got deodorants that were so crudely designed, in such a lethal suspension, that they had to be taken off the market. The medical profession, lethargic on this issue to the utmost degree, rose up and threw them out. I can't tell you the answer except that I would put it down to a degree of 'uterus loathing.' Nobody wants to even consider it.

"The condom has been treated like a custom built motor car. They have tried to make the condom into a fetish object on its own behalf. That is one way of dealing with contraception I suppose, but people are too fetishistic anyway to my mind."

"We've always had the option of sterilization. I think it's a crummy option. For example, I did not want a child until I was thirty some. If you had offered me sterilization in my twenties, I might have accepted it and I would have been heartbroken to discover that it was irreversible in my thirties. The other thing is your fertility is diminishing. It was very easy for you to get pregnant, or make a girl pregnant, when you were starting to have sex. By the time you're about forty you're not such a risk anymore and it seems ridiculous that you have to be totally covered at all times. I like to think that your life could be renewed at any moment."

When I suggested that her anti-contraceptive stand, her views on abstinence and more natural methods of birth control would find favour at the Vatican, Germaine threw back her head and laughed loudly.

"The Vatican would not approve of my telling women to practice polymorphous, perverse sex the way, as human beings, you are capable of doing. They would be horrified."

'But," I asked, "are there any religious considerations on your part?"

"None whatever," she answered. "The church does not consider women's health. That's not why the church says to use the rhythm method. My whole argument is that you should only have the sex that you want. You should use it to get pleasure, which is the exact opposite of the church's teaching, and you shouldn't be half-poisoning yourself to do something that doesn't give you great pleasure and is likely to leave you pregnant and with a whole lot of other problems."

You do not have to agree with every point that Germaine Greer makes to see the value in what she has to say. She is an eloquent woman, strong in her beliefs and perfectly willing to back up her beliefs with facts. Judging from the mail received after the programme aired, viewers were upset by several things: her choice of words, her belief that pleasure is the basis of sexual relations and her recommending the practice of "polymorphous, perverse sex." She represents an extreme. From this extreme each of us can make a personal judgement, decide what is right in our own lives.

It would be a great mistake to argue with Ms. Greer about the declining sexual morés of our age. This is not the basis of her stated opinions. Health is. Her stance is based on the acceptance that everyone is involved in sexual activity, whether we like it or not, whether they are married or not, young or old. Too many women are frightened. They don't want to get pregnant in the current relationship. They don't know what the contraceptive alternatives are. To make matters worse the viable alternatives all have their inherent problems, even dangers.

Philosophical conversations will not help the pregnant fourteen year old or the thirty year old who is constantly fighting infection after taking the pill for ten years. The key again, is information. From information we have choice.

Put the complaints aside. Suspend your prejudices concerning the particulars Germaine Greer expresses. Look, instead at the underlying premise. Sexual relationships, without love, without spiritual involvement, without genuine caring, are not worth it. "It's sort of low level, friendly, cool-out, boring sex, like having a cup of tea or a glass of water or something."

She would, I think, judge that there are two essential factors involved: an understanding of the clinical alternatives and a certain understanding of self. That is what made this programme a *Man Alive*.

Anthony Bloom

IS LIFE
WORTH LIVING?

*We have within ourselves a God-Shaped emptiness
and nothing else but God can fill it.*

Man Alive has often investigated what might be described as
"gentler" subjects, subjects which are contemplative rather than
active. In the course of a lifetime a person will reflect on such
things as the universe, or the relationship of God to man, or simply
ask the question "why." No answer is expected, but this kind of
philosophical thought has led many to a deeper understanding
of themselves and of the world which surrounds them. It is with
the hope of prompting this kind of thought that these programmes
are produced.

It was our good fortune to meet Metropolitan Anthony Bloom,
head of the Russian Orthodox Church in England. Through this
gentle man, many of these philosophical thoughts were expressed.
Bloom is a rare mixture of theologian and realist. Never is the
listener able to forget that this man has lived in the same world as
you or me, yet he is able to put into words these difficult con-

cepts, based on his firm belief and academic knowledge.

Anthony Bloom was born in Lausanne, Switzerland in 1914. He spent most of his childhood in Russia, then Persia where his father, a member of the Imperial Diplomatic Corps, was stationed. After the Russian Revolution his family moved to the west, although retaining the traditions of the Russian people. Bloom describes himself at this time as an unbeliever. He says, "I had no contact either with the gospel or Christ in a personal way, even less perhaps with the church. I was an unbeliever as far as believing was concerned and very anti-church as far as going to church was concerned."

When he was fifteen his attitude changed. He became a member of a church affiliated boys group and therefore became exposed to the gospel. He was sufficiently interested to ask to borrow his mother's Bible. While reading the gospel according to Mark, he became aware of a presence. "I (knew) that Christ was standing on the other side of the desk and (the impression) was so clear and so certain that I looked up the way one looks around in the street when one has the impression that someone is looking at your back. I saw nothing, perceived nothing with my senses but the certainty was so great that I knew that I had met Christ alive and if I had met Christ alive then all the gospel was true."

This experience was to lay the foundation of a profound faith as well as give this child meaning in life. Bloom decided to give himself one year to find this meaning and if there was none, to commit suicide, 'because there was no point in living an aimless existence." The experience gave dimension to his life. He envisioned a God "who was on the scale of man, capable of understanding everything, but calling men to be on his scale ultimately and not just a very remarkable species of animality."

Bloom completed his education in France, becoming a medical doctor. While a surgeon in a Paris hospital, World War II broke out. Bloom served as a senior officer until the fall of France when he became active in the resistance movement. In 1943 he took his monastic vows while still practicing medicine.

For many people science and religion are at odds. Their basic assumptions at first seem to negate each other. There was no such problem in Bloom's life.

"I never tried to make the Bible into a book of natural history. I never tried to check scientific knowledge by religious presumptions. I always felt that even if we cannot always see the ways in which things link, the knowledge of the world in which we live is the knowledge of God and his works. They cannot conflict. If one has intellectual and moral integrity one must follow each line in its own right. My spiritual life went along one line; my intellectual life only enriched what I knew of God.''

In 1948 Bloom was ordained into the priesthood. He then moved to England where he devoted all his time to religion. In 1958 he was consecrated bishop, rising to the rank of Metropolitan of the Russian Orthodox Church in 1966.

I first met Anthony Bloom in 1973. I was immediately struck by the intensity of his gaze. This was obviously a man who viewed life as a serious matter. His figure is at once imposing and generous, an austere outer visage with great depth lying within.

The subject of our first interview was suffering. The Christian concept of suffering being redemptive is perplexing. It is difficult to believe that any good can come from the pain we see experienced by all around us. Why then is it held as an admirable state?

Anthony Bloom was anxious to explain that suffering in itself achieved nothing. ''It may be a curse and a hell without any issue out of it, but when endured in the name of love, for the sake of love, ultimately for the sake of God and of man, in a personal way, it is redemptive.''

I wasn't sure that the church made this distinction clear and that many people, therefore, had missed that particular point feeling they could indeed, reach salvation through suffering.

Bloom agreed, ''I think lots of people miss this point and many other points, both in the gospel and in life. It's easier to work out a world outlook in which enduring suffering is meaningful than to say that enduring suffering is nothing if I do not love. Loving is infinitely more difficult than enduring. Enduring is a passive state. Once suffering is inflicted it takes courage and determination to undergo it with love.''

As I listened to Bloom I couldn't help remembering my interview with Elie Wiesel. He spoke of the Jewish concept of suffering as being abhorrent to their faith. Life, he said, should be a celebration. I mentioned this to Bloom.

He said, ''Ideally, yes, life should be a celebration, but in the face of a world of disharmony, of hatred, of mutual antagonism, of contrast and opposition, suffering is inevitable and it can be turned into a redemptive experience.''

Death is, in Bloom's opinion, the full measure of suffering. Even in this ultimate state he sees some hope.

''If we really believe that God is a God of the living, that through him everyone is alive, that there is a future which is eternity, then the death of a person is only a moment of separation, a separation with a difference. If that person is truly alive in God and so are you, there is a present and a future, not only a past. The rest of your life can be marked by the life of that person now in God's keeping. You may be, on earth, the continuation of all that was good in that person or the undoing of all that was wrong. That is an active participation in the eternal destiny."

Perhaps one of the most damaging things a person can do is to pretend, to live in a dream world, to believe that all is well when it is not or to fear a time when suffering will come. The love of which Bloom speaks, when fully realized, would equip a person to face suffering, could in fact build character.

"Pain as pain cannot build character. A daring, a courageous way of facing pain does. For example, in present day medicine people turn to a doctor to alleviate the slightest pain because they assume they should never be in pain. The result is that they can face pain less and less and when there is no pain they can't face the fear. In the end they live in pain although there is no real pain yet.

"Suffering can be a testing of a person, a refining of him, provided you face it creatively, daringly, in order to make something of your life and of your person. If you face it passively, if you simply endure slavishly, it will simply make you a slave, more subservient and more afraid and that is not the aim of it."

I felt, at the conclusion of the interview, that I had been speaking to a friend. It was hard to imagine I had known this man only a few days. His concern and his ability to touch nerves so deeply buried was disarming. I was sure that a lot could be learned about humanity from him.

Not surprisingly the viewers seemed to agree. The reaction to the programme was extremely positive with many requests to have Bloom return. The staff of *Man Alive* were also enthusiastic so arrangements were made to interview Bloom again later in that same year.

The first topic we discussed was a counterpoint to the previous interview. From the depths of suffering, we entered the realm of joy.

It seemed to me that the distinction between joy and happiness was as difficult a concept as the redemptive value of suffering. What was the difference?

"Joy," said Bloom, "is an inward state. Pleasure and happiness are things that happen. Something which is pleasurable can awaken in us a feeling of joy that was dormant. Joy is a sense of life with abundance. You can't buy joy. It is there always, though it may be sleeping. We can find it in a child. Life is bubbling up and joy is there. Joy precedes happiness or pleasure.''

It was evident that Bloom felt joy was innate, something you are born with, yet I sensed that it was something people searched for all their lives, or, were they searching for more temporary pleasures?

"Very often," Bloom said, "we look for products of replacement. I think what is characteristic of joy is that it cannot be taken away from you. What is characteristic of happiness, pleasure, elation, ecstasy, rapture and all these things, is that they come to you from outside. You only respond. Joy belongs to you.''

We often think that the opposite of joy is sorrow. I asked Bloom if he felt this was true.

"I think that lifelessness is the opposite of joy. When things go dull, dim, lifeless, meaningless, then joy is gone.''

Bloom felt strongly about the concept of Christian joy, the sense of Christmas, Easter and Pentecost. I wasn't as sure as he that it remained an element of modern day worship. "The Christians of today seem a grim lot. Very often as you stand at the front of a church and look down at them singing Hallelujah or Joy To the World, they're gritting their teeth and looking pretty sour. Where has this Christian joy gone?''

Bloom looked up, surprised and said, "I think you should have been here for Easter night. There was a great sense of suspense and excitement and joy about the resurrection.''

Another thing that bothered me was the Christmas season, the "joyous" season, yet all around us depression and suicide, a time of loneliness. Why had this happened?

"I think the problem," said Bloom, "is that we have made Christmas a 'family feast' so that everyone who is not of the family is simply kicked out. It no longer has the quality of an event that binds heaven and earth together, all the family of men. We say glory to God on high and on earth peace and good will towards men. Well, glory to God remains, because we can't touch it. Peace on earth is more doubtful. As to good will toward men, as long as we consider Christmas a family feast, there will be no good will.''

I mentioned to Bloom that I have often wondered if we expect to feel joyous at Christmas because it is the joyous season and when we don't feel joyous we feel guilty for not feeling the joy of Christmas.

Bloom responded, "I think you must have a very sensitive conscience to feel that. The majority of people concentrate on turkey."

Since the beginning of the Christian faith, the church and its members have had difficulty in characterizing Jesus Christ. We felt that this might be a good time to ask Bloom to illuminate the image.

I asked him if he felt the gospels gave us an accurate picture of Jesus.

"The gospels were not aimed at giving us an historical Jesus in the sense of modern history. The aim was to make us perceive that, though he was genuinely, truly, a man he was in fact the son of God."

"I have always related to Jesus very well at moments when he was very human, when he must have been disappointed. I see him as a great man, a unique man, a perfect man. Is that not enough?"

Bloom was adamant. "Christ's divinity is absolutely the central message of the gospels. If you want to be a Christian in the sense in which the apostles were, you must recognize this, though it doesn't mean that you are alien to Christ if you have not."

There is a logical difficulty inherent in the acceptance of Christ's divinity. If divine, how could he be human? If human how could he be divine?

Bloom saw no difficulty with the dichotomy.

"He was a man without evil in him, but with all the problems of facing and overcoming evil. His was a progressive, real growth, a human growth while at the same time the way of attaining complete harmony with God. He asks us to try to be more like him."

"But here is a man who is said to walk on water, raise people from the dead and he's asking us to be like him? How can we?"

"We can relate not to the walking on water or the raising of the dead, which to put it in an inelegant way is a by-product, like a book is the by-product of a writer or like a piece of music to the composer. What matters is the music within the man or the sense of the power of the word within the other. He was God who came into our world to teach us something on the one hand and to make us perceive with all the intensity of an emotional response and intellectual understanding how much men matter to God. He involved his son in that way, for the sake of man. Jesus was not simply a man who achieved his own personal goals. He is primarily God who came into the world to speak to us, to be in our midst."

"What was the central message of Jesus?"

"I think love of a very peculiar type and quality, peculiar because it is a love of giving not taking."

Bloom's final statement seems to me to define why Jesus Christ, however perceived, has remained important through the years. "If the central message was love, then He is indeed a man for today."

In 1976 we again travelled to England. This was a time of great alienation in our western culture. We had made it through the turbulent sixties, full of its hopes and its battles and were now well into the seventies. Many of the questions posed were not answered and people were feeling lost. They were feeling the results of lives stripped of purpose. It was our feeling that Anthony Bloom could provide insight into this problem, perhaps suggest a way in which people could again find meaning.

This show was unusual in that the entire programme was shot within a moving vehicle. We had hoped to interview Bloom in various parks, showing people in the background in order to lend life to his words. Unfortunately, Anthony Bloom has a severe allergy to grass, making it impossible for him to spend much time outside. We therefore achieved the active background by conducting the interview within the controlled environment of a car.

"As we travel through a city like London and see all the people walking and driving cars, they seem to have a sense of being cut off, an aloneness."

"It is not enough to be involved physically with other people," said Bloom. "Meeting people, talking to people, working with people, may very well only enhance your sense of loneliness. People have lost the ability to communicate. They have lost the ability to express themselves because vocabulary has become shallow, because images have become conventional, because no real effort is made for a deep, intense, intellectual elaboration of thought and a real attempt at expressing interior experience in adequate words has become impossible.

"Understanding has also become shallow because people are afraid of commitment. When a sick person being asked, 'How are you today?' answers, 'All right thank you,' we're too happy to hear anything more. We don't look into the eyes of this person. We don't see the anguish. We don't hear the tremor of the voice. We don't see the obvious signs of disease, a covering lie.

"To hear and to see means to get committed. We have become timid. We do not dare live in an adventurous way. We are prepared to establish promiscuous relationships that do not last, but not love relationships that are forever. The result is that people are lonely because they know perfectly well that they will be dropped at the moment when they are too difficult or superfluous or no longer interesting. I think this is a very important feature of our time — fear of commitment and inability to communicate either by expressing one's self or by being attentive towards what the other one has got to say.''

''There seems to be no age barrier to this sense of loneliness. As you look around you see people of every age, from all walks of life suffering from it.'' I observed.

''It's not a new phenomenon that the young feel lonely. There is a period in everyone's development when he becomes aware of his uniqueness, of being a person, and begins to doubt that anyone can understand him or her. And there is a sense of loneliness which derives from this.

''I think that in western civilization the old are in a very bad position because it seems to be a tradition in the west that when two young people marry, they set up a home apart from the old home. The parents, the grandparents are not involved, in the life of the new house. When they grow a little bit older, if they are in the care of their children, so often they are told, 'You find life difficult now; we have found a lovely place for you. You'll be looked after.' And they get everything except affection. They are put aside in an almost definitive way. That's another type of loneliness.

''And then there is the loneliness of so many people in our society, because of this compartmented aspect of life in which people live in a bedsitter, in a small flat, in a hotel room. They go to work and to the people who work with them, they are a function but not a person.

''We may discover after years that a person is human, while we thought he was just either a boss or a typist. And this is an extremely grave thing because it's a denial of personality as it were. You don't exist. Your function exists, you're totally interchangeable. And within this system, however much you relate to people, you know that people don't relate to you in a definite way. If you disappear you will simply be missed until someone else steps into your shoes.''

''This time of loneliness or feeling of worthlessness, this void has been called 'the dark night of the soul.' You say it can be a creative time. Then this void must be faced and worked through?''

I asked.

"You can't avoid it because there is no path you can follow. At least no known path to you. Otherwise, it would just be a patch of darkness on a road which is secure. Why I said it can be a hopeful experience is that I believe if we have courage to face it, and the daring to face it, we may realize that this void implies the possibility of fulfillment and that darkness implies life. The sense that life has no meaning for me, implies that within me there is something testifying to the fact that there can be meaning.

"There is a remarkable passage you certainly know in the Old Testament when Moses asks to see the glory of God, and he is told, you cannot do that. But it will pass by, and you will see me from the back. Well, if you imagine the scene, Moses wishes to be confronted with the fullness of a divine radiance, the divine splendour. He can't do it at the stage where he is. But what he can say is that God has passed and is going away. And his only chance is to follow...to follow and catch up with him. And I think it's an image that should be remembered. Of course, when we are in the grip of this meaninglessness, of the despair, of the wish to commit suicide, of the desire never to have been and certainly not to be, then we don't reason it out that way. Yet, we can sense in the void, the emptiness, the despair in the face of nonsense, that there is within us a proclamation that there must be meaning.

"I think the root of suicide and death is not simply the fact that there is no answer. That would be an intellectual and logical conclusion. But first and foremost, the fact that people are so lonely. There is a great deal one can endure together with others: the war, a terminal illness, when someone stands by and is prepared to go all the way together with you. People commit suicide at the point when they feel they can't endure it any more because there will be no end to it. Something which entails physical pain or moral agony, which you could not conceivably endure for years or ages, you may face on short-term basis. I remember a child of nine whom I met when I was a medical student, who was afflicted with a terminal illness, extremely painful, who struck us by his serenity, composure, which was far beyond his age and certainly alien to his condition. We asked how it was that he could face his pain and his coming death, since he was aware of it. Calmly he said, 'I have learned not to rehearse yesterday's suffering, and not to anticipate tomorrow's.' And so he lived within the day and he divided the day into portions which were small enough to be endured.

"In situations of extreme tragedy, like the one which people had to face in concentration camps and still have in certain countries, the rate of suicide is extremely small because the problem is survival and people know from within a physical experience, not only an imaginative approach, what death means. And so they are not prepared to go into death lightly or at a moment of crisis, because they know its finality. They see it around them and they feel it within themselves."

"So, if a person comes to you and says 'I am having feelings of worthlessness. I'm trying to figure out why I am here, questioning my whole existence. I'm just a speck in the universe, what does it matter?' What would you say to them to help them work through these ultimate questions?"

"We all are just specks in the universe, very small ones, very frail ones, if we see ourselves against the background of galaxies or simply in the context of a car that can run us over. But, at the same time, when we look inward we see that there is in this speck a depth which is not measurable, which can be spoken of in terms of profundity, and which is so vast and so deep, that whatever we try to fill it with, we can't do it. We try to pour knowledge into it and there is still hunger, thirst and emptiness, beauty also, love also. And we discover at a certain moment that the vastness is such, that unless there is something else, we will remain empty. To use a phrase of Michael Ramsey, which you can find also in Jung, we have within ourselves a God-shaped emptiness and nothing else but God can fill it. And in that sense, outwardly, while infinitely small and insignificant, inwardly, we have all the measurements which love gives us. Even in human relationships we are worthless until we are discovered by someone for whom we become the whole universe. And in terms of God, our worth is all the love and all the death of Christ. So we cannot say whether we are worthless or not, unless we define first our criteria. If it is in terms of outer criteria, the vastness of the universe on the one hand, or the usefulness for a task on the other hand, we may find one thing too small. But if you think in terms of a relationship, in terms of love, then you may have an absolute value. And I think that in this struggle for the discovery of one's value, the ultimate is the discovery that one is of infinite and absolute value in terms of love."

"You feel that every life has a purpose?" I asked.

"I think, outwardly, it may be argued one way or another. If, by purpose, you mean achieve great things on earth, put a seal on great events, be known and spoken of in newspapers or the media, no. If you mean by this, that in the process of living we can grow to a full stature of beauty, become great and become vast enough for God, I will say, yes, everyone without any exception. And, say a man like Brother Lawrence, who was a mystic of the Middle Ages, who spent all his life doing nothing but cooking in his monastery, but doing it with love and as an act of worship, achieved a quality of human being, which is far greater than a number of others who seemingly played a great role in history, and in the end seemed to be so small, because we discover after twenty years or a hundred years, how much vanity there was and how little greatness.''

After every appearance by Anthony Bloom on *Man Alive* we receive requests for transcripts of his remarks. After this one there was such a demand we had to have bulk quantities printed. Viewers appreciated being able to read his remarks over and over again.

It is difficult for either the camera or the transcript to show the warm and humourous Anthony Bloom. Indeed, with his piercing black eyes, long black beard and flowing black cassock he appears as some benevolent Rasputin. But to watch him tenderly cuddling the babies of his parishioners after the Sunday service or hear him laugh and joke with the noonday regulars at a working class pub where he enjoys a 'pie and a pint' is to understand another side to this amazing man.

His health at this time is failing and I'm sure the millions who have read his books and articles and heard him on numerous radio and television broadcasts all over the world are praying that he be given the strength to continue sharing his wisdom, his faith and his love for a long time to come.

SCIENCE
OR NO SCIENCE,
THEY BELIEVED.

Through the visual reality that images present,
believers can come closer to the invisible
realities of their faith.

Viewers wrote for many years suggesting the Shroud of Turin as
a possible topic for *Man Alive*. The subject was always dismissed
as rather trivial. For some, the Shroud falls into the same category
as the weeping Madonna, or stigmata. The overall opinion of the
staff was that faith is as strong without belief in relics, so why
highlight that particular facet of devotion? A Roman Catholic
bishop once told me "Why don't you throw all the relics into one
show and have done with it?"

A few changes came in 1978 which made the Shroud a more
compelling subject. For the first time in thirty years it was going
on public display, thus arousing the attention of the media from
around the world. There was also controversy over the scientific
testing. Which methods would be allowed? Would the results
become public? These combined elements were irresistible.

Man Alive was the obvious production unit to attend because of the religious questions involved. But it was not simply the religious implications which drew us there. We were also reporting a news event as well as helping to unravel a mystery. If a forgery, the Shroud would be one of the biggest hoaxes ever perpetrated on mankind. If not, it was probably the first time faith ever looked to scientific testing for proof. Either way here was a story. But underlying that story were the people, the people who travelled thousands of miles for one glimpse of the Shroud, who were anxious, even desperate to have their faith reaffirmed by gazing at what they considered to be the face of their saviour. But what of this Shroud?

This remarkable piece of stained cloth is fourteen feet three inches long and three feet seven inches wide. It can be traced historically back to 1353, when it was presented as the burial shroud of Christ, to the church at Lirey, France by one Geoffrey de Charny, who had acquired it as a spoil of war. When the church refused to accept the authenticity of the relic, Geoffrey's granddaughter Margaret took possession and finally gave it to the Dukes of Savoy in 1453. It has remained with the House of Savoy since that day and has passed to the present owner King Umberto II. Prior to 1353 the history of the Shroud is very murky and highly speculative. If any fraud took place it had to have been done before that date.

Ian Wilson, an Oxford history graduate, theorized in his book *The Shroud of Turin* that it is one and the same as the most celebrated icon of Christ, the Holy Mandylion or the Edessa cloth. This fabric was brought to Edessa during the first century by Abgar V who reigned from 4 BC to 50 AD. But as yet no real proof has surfaced to support this theory. Since the Shroud's historical pedigree before the 1350's is all conjecture it seems logical that scientific dating methods should be used to help prove its authenticity.

This is not as easy as it sounds. The Archbishop of Turin, Anastasio Ballestrero, and the commission for the Holy Shroud are slow to give the green light to conclusive scientific examination and jealously guard any existent test results.

A crucial and most controversial test would be the Carbon 14 dating process. One of the best and most accurate laboratories was at the University of Rochester in New York.

Dr. Harry Gove, the director, told me that if they were given a piece of the Shroud the size of a finger nail they could date it within fifty to one hundred years of its age.

Carbon 14 dating, or radio carbon dating, is the determination

170

of the age of any organic substance by measuring the radioactivity of its carbon content. The measurable level of radioactivity in carbon deteriorates at a constant rate and loses potency after 5,568 years.

Gove and his team of American and Canadian scientists happily showed us through their laboratory explaining the Carbon 14 process, obviously looking forward to working on the Shroud.

Public interest in the Shroud was becoming more intense as the exhibition date neared.

A film *Silent Witness* produced in England by David Rolfe was drawing larger audiences than *Saturday Night Fever*. Rolfe told *Man Alive*, "I rather suspected that if we started a film investigation into the subject we would find that the Shroud was a fake. The whole process took some three and one half years. During that time our research just grew and grew. In the end not only did I not find a forgery but the whole experience had a tremendous impact on me. I had started out skeptical, not only about the Shroud, but religion generally. I was very much a disinterested agnostic. In the process of making the film I found myself a believing Christian. I don't know how it happened but it did happen, and I'm very glad of it."

The anatomical accuracy of the image on the cloth greatly impressed Rolfe. "You have to remember," he said, "that the image was there long before Leonardo da Vinci or Michaelangelo were even born and yet the accuracy of the anatomy is greater than even they were able to show."

The accuracy was also emphasized by London's Professor James Cameron, one of the world's most outstanding criminal investigators and forensic scientists. He told us, "All my medico-legal assumptions are done solely on the premise that it is in fact, a photograph. How it became a photograph is a matter beyond my knowledge. It is obviously of considerable interest to the theologians, but from a purely scientific aspect, and the medico-legal aspect in particular, I prefer not to enter into it."

Standing beside a large photograph of the Shroud and using a male skeleton for comparison, Professor Cameron pointed out some fascinating evidence for our cameras.

"When we note the muscle stiffness or rigor we can say that rigor was established when the body was placed in the Shroud. In other words, he had been dead three to five hours prior to being placed in the Shroud. When the image took, or whenever the body photographed itself for want of a better terminology, one cannot be sure, except that it obviously happened within the thirty-six hours it took for the rigor to wear off.

"The face indicates extensive bruising and swelling on one side as if it had come into contact against a very hard object. It's similar to what one sees in a boxer, or somebody who has been mugged. There are certain aspects which I would like to draw your attention to, particularly the marks on the back and top of the head and the front of the face."

At this point Dr. Cameron showed us some thorns of the genus *spina christi* grown in Kew Gardens.

"You must realize," he said, "that these are about a third of the size of those they would find in Palestine, but a crown of such thorns could well penetrate the skin and cause the rivulets of blood which are depicted in this image."

He remarked that artists over the years had usually shown Christ's crown of thorns as a circulet, but he believes the image shows an actual crown, shaped much like a cap, that had gone right over the head. Dr. Cameron's examination of the back of the image, an area which normally receives less attention, was equally interesting.

"The back shows the marks of the scourging we have read about in the Gospels. He was scourged in the classical way, with a flagram. The Roman flagram had a sort of dumbell at either end of a bit of rope, similar to a cat o'nine tails, only with two or three tails, each with two pellets. So the marks we see on this image are in actual fact a collection of small dots in several places. There are one hundred and twenty collections like this which indicate this body was subjected to one hundred and twenty strokes."

Dr. Cameron added that had the victim been a Roman citizen he would have been beaten with rods, not whipped with a flagram. Also the inflictors of the punishment were not of the Jewish faith as their law forbade more than forty lashes. He pointed out that the other important medico-legal finding was that this particular man was flagellated before the crossbeam was placed on his shoulders. If a heavy crossbeam is placed across the shoulder blades, and is carried for some distance it would leave a definite bruise. This image according to Dr. Cameron did indeed show a bruise, but within that bruise are marks of the flagram. Since it was usual to whip prisoners while they carried their cross the evidence here strongly corresponds with the gospel account of a prior scourging which, Pilate hoped, would in itself satisfy the multitude.

"Those of us who have dissected or inspected many bodies, have at least learned to doubt. Those who are ignorant of anatomy and do not take the trouble to attend to it at all, are in no doubt at all. In other words, all I can say after all my examinations is that this Turin relic might be Christ's own burial cloth, not that it is."

The Shroud would be on exhibition from August 27th to October 8th, the longest ever in modern times.

Turin, a pleasant city in Northwest Italy on the River Po, would see its population of one million twenty thousand swell by over three million in one of the largest pilgrimages in history. On the last two days of the event a Congress of Studies sponsored by the International Centre for Sindonology (Sindona means Shroud) would take place. Here, experts from all over the world would discuss the scientific, historical and theological research that had turned up in the past few years. Hopefully, some scientific tests would be allowed in those final hours before the relic would be returned to its triple locked, asbestos lined, iron chest in the sepulcher in the Cathedral of St. John the Baptist.

I flew to Turin at the height of the event. My producer had arrived a few days earlier and had lined up a number of people for me to meet and interview. The city itself with its arched stone canopies and cobbled streets seemed to be in a calm, business as usual, mood. A few stores carried souvenir replicas of the Shroud, and bookshops naturally displayed Shroud editions, but generally local interest seemed at a low ebb. I asked the *il cameriere* who served my breakfast if he planned on viewing the *sindone*. He said he had seen it once on television in 1973 and that was good enough for him.

At the Cathedral square it was a different story. A sea of people, at the rate of one hundred per wave, surged up the specially constructed ramps to spill noiselessly into the church's darkened interior. From all over the world they came to this once in a lifetime event; young backpackers from Germany and the Netherlands, still wearing hiking boots and carrying staffs, American and Japanese tourists harnessed in cameras and cassette tape recorders, old black-habited nuns, their fingers stiffly worrying the familiar beads, being fairly lifted along by young novices whose faces glowed in anticipation of what lay ahead.

Our crew was given special permission to set up in front of the altar just a few feet from the Shroud in order to film it in detail. Afterwards I found the experience was heightened by going through with the crowd and seeing it from their perspective. The procession remained about ten deep, moving slowly and orderly. The babble of conversation and laughter turned to a murmur upon entering the cathedral, then a hushed silence approaching the altar. The Shroud was stretched out to its full length and mounted in a case made of thick bazooka-proof glass. There had been concern about possible terrorist activity during the exhibition. Turin is the home of the notorious Red Brigade.

Every detail of the shroud was perfectly visible. The linen itself is ivory coloured and in remarkably good condition where it is not burned and stained from a fire at Chambery in 1532 and by the water used to douse the flames.

The image, faint and sepia in tone, is two impressions of a male body, front and back, head to head. Having seen many pictures of the image I was at first disappointed that the markings were so dim. Then I realized, what thousands of others had realized before me. One of the phenomena of this relic is that the greatest clarity emerges through photography. The shroud impression is apparently a negative image, so, by making a photographic negative, the picture becomes a positive of the scene.

This was discovered by a startled Seconda Pia, lawyer by profession, photographer by avocation, in 1898 when he became the first person to photograph the shroud.

On May 28th of that year Pia was given an hour to set up his cumbersome equipment and to take a photograph. At 11 p.m. Pia exposed his first plate for a fourteen minute time-exposure. At midnight he finished exposing his second plate for twenty minutes and headed for his dark room. There the image on his negative began coming through the chemical bath in startling depth and clarity. Pia almost collapsed.

He wrote later, "Closed up in my dark room, I experienced such an intense emotion when I saw for the first time the Holy Face appear on the plate with such clearness, that I remained frozen."

To the naked eye the image is clearer when viewed from twenty to thirty feet distant as it was by the crowd in the Cathedral. It almost disappears any closer.

The people inch their way along, each very much absorbed in their own feelings. Some fall to their knees in veneration, tears streaming down many faces. Lips move in silent prayer. Many just stare and stare, cheeks glowing and eyes bright with adoration. Guides gently but firmly urge the mass through. Some pause at the exit for a long, last look and a murmured prayer before stepping back out into the bright Italian sunshine.

It would be impossible to ignore such raw emotion. After all, this is where the importance of the Shroud lies, with the people.

Every person who passed by was affected by the experience. I spoke to many of them as they left the exhibition.

A woman from San Francisco was so overcome with emotion she could hardly speak. Through tears she told me, "There's no doubt. That image is the image of Jesus Christ. Oh, without a doubt it is the Shroud of Jesus. I just give thanks to God for the opportunity of being here."

A Canadian man told me, "It's like looking at someone I really love. For me He is God. Jesus of Nazareth is God. To look at that face on the Shroud is a bit like looking at the face of God. I hope that when I die I'll see that face with his eyes open. He is my Lord."

While thousands of pilgrims were battling with their emotions after viewing the Shroud, a battle of a different kind was taking place at the Scientific Congress. Professor Harry Gove from Rochester was pushing hard for his Carbon 14 testing permission.

"We have developed a technique in the past year and a half which detects Carbon 14 from very small samples; samples that are one thousand times smaller than the conventional technique. One would require only a single wet thread twenty centimetres long. That would produce enough carbon to make a date," he said.

To everyone's surprise Monsignor Cotino, secretary to the Archbishop of Turin and member of the Commission of the Holy Shroud, claimed that Carbon 14 testing had not been requested. This was hotly denied by the scientists, but Cotino stood firm. "Let me be sincere," he said. "These tests have not been anticipated, nor have they been requested. I have already told the press this. There is no hope for these tests because of serious problems of accuracy. But you are young. Have faith. In the year 2000 or 2050 these tests will be done then."

Later outside the congress I chatted briefly with Monsignor Cotino about the apparent mix up. I explained that Professor Gove was under the impression his request had been made clear several months ago. As we were talking, Professor Gove came near. I invited him over and invited Cotino to meet and talk with him. Cotino became very angry. He ignored Gove's outstretched hand and said, "I had the pleasure of seeing this gentleman today for the first time in my life. I am now going to say good bye." With that he strode into the crowd and disappeared.

Responsibility for the safety and sanctity of the Shroud rested solely with Anastasio Ballestrero the newly appointed Archbishop of Turin. We managed to set up a meeting with him in the large, ornate Bishop's Palace. Ballestrero is short, very round and brusque of manner. At this particular time he was thought by many to be a prime candidate for the papal office.

When Pope Paul died in August, Ballestrero's name had been mentioned, but his chances thought slim because he had not yet been made a cardinal. Though still not a cardinal in October when John Paul I died, his name was pushed hard by some Roman clergy as they suddenly faced the distinct possibility of a non-Italian pope.

On this particular weekend in October many cardinals were arriving in Rome to prepare for the Conclave the following week. Some made the extra journey to Turin to see the Holy Shroud during its exhibition and, I imagine, to get a closer look at their papabile.

Ballestrero speaks no English. Working through an interpreter I asked him if he was concerned about the authenticity of the Shroud. He said, "If the Shroud is a fake it is not an intentional fake. It is true that there is insufficient historical documentation for the Shroud, but the question of its authenticity shouldn't concern the church directly. It is a concern of science. The church venerates the image on the Shroud, as it venerates many other images. Through the visual reality that images present, believers can come closer to the invisible realities of their faith. As far as I am concerned the question of the authenticity of the Shroud is simply left to science."

Time was growing short for both the scientists and the spectators. The exhibition hours at the cathedral were extended to accommodate the huge crowds, but finally the great carved doors were closed and the public viewing was over.

Early the next morning I stood in the Cathedral square and watched the workmen dismantling the ramps while others began washing down the cobblestones. It was hard to imagine that three million people had just gathered there. The square was deserted and quiet except for an occasional hammering or a burst of song from one of the workers.

What had really happened here? Had the curious and faithful been privileged to view a priceless icon, "a snapshot of the resurrection," or had they simply seen an old piece of linen, cleverly forged? Perhaps the current round of scientific tests will uncover new evidence about the origin of the Shroud and the image it contains. But since most of the scientists I had met were believers already, could their findings truly be trusted? Would the commission of the Holy Shroud release findings detrimental to their famous cloth? Since Carbon 14 testing was not being allowed would this limited investigation really prove anything? Many of the questions we had prepared at the beginning of the production remained unanswered.

In the early morning hours as I walked through Turin's empty square I found myself troubled. I was quite willing to believe that the Shroud of Turin was indeed the burial cloth of Christ. There was certainly no evidence to prove that it wasn't. But what difference did it make? Surely if one is a Christian the important consideration is the man Jesus, his life, his teachings, his example, not a piece of cloth that he may have been buried in. If proof of miracles is needed to strengthen faith it can't be much of a faith to begin with. But to those people face to face with God it did make a difference. They believed. Science or no science, they believed.

The Shroud of Turin is an intriguing and highly emotional mystery. Like most mysteries, especially those involving faith, it is perhaps better that it remain unsolved.

THE GREAT SPIRIT

*When you think you are equal to the
smallest of God's creations then you can
start talking to your Creator.*

Man Alive has always maintained a continuing concern for Canada's native people. We have filmed several programmes on location with various Indian tribes and organizations.

The underlying theme of these programmes remained constant, to show on television aspects of Indian traditions and beliefs with the hope of creating a better understanding between Canadians. Because of its reputation as a responsible and caring series, the Indians allowed *Man Alive* to view areas of their life not usually open to the media.

In 1975, after a year's preparation, our crew was allowed to film the sacred Morley conference on the Stoney Indian Reserve in Alberta. Navahos, Ojibways, Crees, Apaches and other native people gather there from all over North America to search for ways to strengthen Indian union and to pass on teachings and living techniques to the young.

There was a certain amount of opposition to the media being present. It rained daily and heavily and many saw this as a sign of the Great Spirit's displeasure in having this sacred event interrupted by cameras, lights and microphones. Indeed, on the final day, as the equipment was being packed, the rain stopped and the sun burst through the clouds as if to bless the crew's departure.

For the first time in the seven years the conference had been held, more young people than old attended. Edward Benton, an Ojibway from Milwaukee and one of the founders of AIM, the American Indian Movement, said he believed that the native religion was a great source of strength for both the young and the old.

"I don't think that white people have ever fully understood the mysticism and the spiritualism of the native religion. They could not grasp that simple people living in this Garden of Eden could have any understanding of what God is. They believed us too simple, too unsophisticated, too heathen. We were viewed by many as nothing more than animals. What they didn't know was that we had a communication with the creator and indeed with all of creation."

That same year we took a crew to the Poundmaker reserve in northern Saskatchewan to meet and film Ernest Tootoosis, a spiritual leader of the Cree.

The Poundmaker reserve, with its gently rolling hills, crystal clear creeks, pines and poplars, is a few miles west of North Battleford, an area rich in Canadian history. On this site nearly one hundred years ago, during the Riel Rebellion, the Great Chief Poundmaker defeated a force of militia after several hours of battle. It was one of the last military clashes between Indians and government troops in Canada. However, Poundmaker's fight to win equality for his people did not succeed. He died in captivity and despair. Ernest Tootoosis is a direct descendant of Poundmaker and carries on the struggle of his people. He strongly believes that in the centuries old customs and traditions lie the future of today's Indians.

When asked about his traditional beliefs, an Indian usually does not expound doctrine. He does not discuss theology in the abstract. The natural world about him — the animals, the birds, the plants, the rocks and trees — are elements that define his religion.

Sitting next to Poundmaker's grave, Ernest talked to me about God and creation.

"The way the old people told me the story, it is very close to your Adam and Eve, except the North American Indian never disobeyed in his Garden. When the white man came here in 1492 God was taking care of everything for us. We let him run the business. We didn't have to work like the white man did. God provided our food, in the air, on land and in the water and all we had to do was live in harmony with his creation and respect God above all.

"This is Holy Land where man doesn't disobey God; that is, to live against nature; to build dams, or tear the land; to try and conquer nature. The right hand instruments of God are the sun, the wind, the water and the fire. These are holy, spiritual things."

I asked how one went about treating water and fire and trees as holy things.

"Well, we talk to the river. We thank it for doing its duty. When a spiritual person is travelling and comes to a stream he tells it he is going across. He then wets the top of his head with the water, drinks some and crosses. Then when he is over he turns, thanks the water and the creator."

I walked with Ernest over the hills and valleys of his holy land and admired his obvious gratitude to and respect for nature. He explained the uses for the grass and herbs that grew in proliferation as we chatted about Indian medicine.

"Some of the medicine is in flowers, some in bark and herbs. Some you have to mix together for certain diseases." He handed me a stalk and told me to take a bite and chew. It had an earthy nut-like taste. As we chewed, he explained.

"That is for the heart. People who have high blood pressure take it. You just chew a little bit once or twice a day and it helps bring the trouble out of you."

He kept another root in his pocket.

"This comes from the mountains. My people call it 'the root of life.' When a man gets older, about forty-five or fifty he starts taking this. You can chew it, or smoke it, or put some in your tea. It makes you strong and healthy for a long time.

"These medicines will not work," Ernest reminded me, "unless the Great Spirit gives them the power. The person being treated has to believe too. If we are sincere and ask the Great Spirit for help, then things will happen."

We went to Sliding Hill with Ernest and a couple of his older friends. This average sized hill was so named because Nanabush, the messenger of the Great Spirit, appeared here ages ago and in leaving slid down the hill leaving a scorched, barren trail that remains to this day. It is sacred ground and Ernest and his elders often come here to pray and smoke the pipe.

"When we go to pray first we build a fire which represents the creator. Then we take coals from the fire and burn our sweet grass. The spirit of the sweet grass is the messenger of our thoughts and prayers. When the sweet grass burns we purify ourselves before we start praying. We purify our hands, our mouths, our minds, our hearts, our whole body."

The smouldering sweet grass was passed around and Ernest and his friends directed the smoke over the various parts of their bodies in a quiet, solemn ceremony. The traditional long stemmed pipe was lit with a coal from the fire and held high then slowly pointed in four directions in turn.

"The Creator has told us 'before you pray you will light your pipe and show it to me. Then you will show it to the spirits who are set in the four corners of the universe.' You talk to these spirits, first the east, then the south, then west, then north and then straight above. There are four heavens above us and four earth layers below us and every layer has different spirits. These spirits were given powers to pass on to the Indians on this land. The Indian is a beggar to the Great Spirit. We ask every day for life from the creator through his servants. The servants are told 'never be tired of listening to my children, asking for life.' That's what we do in this pipe ceremony. It's done especially for Nanabush who was a great messenger given to us by the Great Spirit."

On a warm, windy afternoon we visited the remains of a Sun Dance lodge which had been used the previous summer. The Sundance is the most sacred of the Plains Cree rituals.

"This is holy ground," Ernest told me. "My father had a Sun Dance on the same ground here. The Sun Dance would be like going to a cathedral to a white man, I guess, or attending a high mass. It's where we pray for ourselves, our immediate family, our people and all mankind. We ask for a better life in the future and also for our everyday needs."

Ernest told me of stories that had been passed down from generation to generation of miracles and visions that occurred at Sun Dances. I asked if he had personally had any visions here.

"When I was a young man I took part in a Sun Dance and about the second day when I was dancing all of a sudden I saw a buffalo head coming out of that tree. It was a small little head. I could see his eyes moving, his nose was damp and his nostrils were flaring. I danced and watched him. Then I closed my eyes and he was gone. I told the old man who had made the Sun Dance and he said I was blessed to have seen the buffalo."

I asked him if it meant anything to him now.

"I always pray to the spirit of the buffalo for guidance, for help in travelling, help in hunting. I pray to the spirit not the animal. To me the buffalo is a child of God, same as you or me; only he looks different. He walks on four legs. He has a spirit the same as I have because God created him too. That's what I don't understand about the white man. He believes he's the only one with a soul. I don't see how he can pray to God if he thinks he is better than his brother. We were taught to humble ourselves, to think that we are as small as the tiniest ant in the grass. When you think you are equal to the smallest of God's creations then you can start talking to your Creator."

The Sun Dance lodge looked bleak and tattered. Bits of ribbon clung to the poles and fluttered in the wind. It didn't look much like a sacred spot.

"These lodges and this very ground is sacred," said Ernest, "and most Indian people respect that. It looks pretty bare now, because they have been stripped. When the Sun Dance is over everything that is used is left here — our drums, our rattles, our whistles, all personal belongings left to rot back to Mother Earth. But we have some good Christian people, people who believe in the white man's religion, who come and take things away as souvenirs. This is our church, I wonder what the white people would think if I went to Montreal to a cathedral there and took some of the holy crosses off a statue and brought them home. Or what if I were to go to a Toronto graveyard and start digging up the white man's bones and say I want to study them to see what he was like. That's what happens to us. They come down here and start digging. It doesn't matter to them that these are holy things."

Despite his sadness about the white man's ways, Ernest did not seem bitter or suspicious. As my visits to his reserve and to his home continued for several days I met his family and friends, shared his food, exchanged recipes with his daughter and was accepted with great warmth and hospitality. One day as we sat on the shore of a small lake, called Manitou Lake by the Indians, he showed me his most prized possession. It was a small bag made from buffalo skin containing a few well-worn stones.

"These stones have been handed down for generations. We don't know how many, on my father's side. The bag is usually opened only once a year. It was opened this summer, but I'll open it for you so you can see."

He shook the stones into his hand, held them reverently for a moment as he silently prayed and then passed them over to me. They were of various sizes and smooth, almost soft, to the touch.

"That stone," he said pointing to the largest one which was about the size of a small walnut, "produces little stones every once in a while. And this one was about the size of a jellybean when it was given to me, and now it's twice that big. The first stone I had, my oldest son is now carrying it in Vancouver. When you look at these stones you can see faces that no one else can see. They are very sacred to us. They are messengers from our Creator."

I handed the stones back. Ernest lit some sweet grass and, as the smoke curled around his hand, explained that he was purifying them before returning them to the buffalo bag.

I asked Ernest if he thought it was important for the young people to return to their ancient beliefs.

"Yes, I do, because that is what an Indian is, a spiritual person. Before the white man came we were very spiritual. We believed in God and his creations and lived in harmony with them. And unless we do that now we are not Indian anymore. Our young people should return to those beliefs and at the same time use the white man's education. Let's play the white man's own game and develop our education to his level, but restore our spiritual power from the Creator. I myself believe that we were a much better people before the white man came here. Maybe we didn't have cars or anything, but we were very rich in spiritual life. I pray that our young people will recapture that spiritual life again."

Now and again, often in the midst of a very hectic schedule, the phone will ring and Ernest's deep, slow voice will ask how I am and what sort of weather we're having. As we chat I'm transported back again to those rolling Saskatchewan hills of birch trees and sweet grass on the Poundmaker reserve where Ernest Tootoosis lives at peace and in harmony with his Creator.

The land is an integral part of the native Indian's very existence. It is more than just something to travel or build on. It is their source of life, or as the Nishga say, their "mother." So, when the government tried to buy the 5,750 square miles of the Nass Valley deep in Northwestern British Columbia the Nishga response was, "This land is not for sale."

In the fall of 1977 we visited the Nishga to talk with them about their land and their beliefs.

The Nishgas are wise in the ways of the white man, using education and the law courts to achieve their rights while, at the same time, relying on their old traditions and beliefs to bolster their claims. There is no doubt in their mind that the land was given to them by God. They have taken their case to Victoria, Ottawa and in 1913 to the King in London, England. But when sitting on the edge of the valley peering at the misty heights of Mount Clou the case for the Nishgas really makes sense. Chief Hubert MacMillan told me of his people's early beginnings.

"That mountain you see there is the one that saved our people from the flood. When the flood came our people stayed close to the mountain. They piled all their belongings onto rafts and rose up the side of the mountain with the water. There is a crevice that runs down the mountain side and our people wedged logs into the crevice and tied the rafts to them in order to stay close. The rains stopped finally and the river went down. A rainbow appeared in the sky. Now when our people see the rainbow they think of the flood and how we were saved."

I asked if this flood was the same one described in the Old Testament.

"Yes it is," he answered. "Only here we have the proof. The logs are still wedged in the crevice all the way up the mountain. They are petrified but they are still there."

When we were filming our programme a sixty foot totem pole was being carved to be erected in front of their new school at Aiyansh, one of four villages along the Nass river where over 2,500 Nishga live.

It is said the carving of totem poles began here about one hundred and eighty years ago. Pictures taken sixty years ago show nearly fifty poles still standing in the area. They were chopped down by the Nishgas in a burst of religious fervour around 1918.

The new one was being carved by Eli Gosnell, a master carver and a hereditary Nishga chieftain. The pole was to commemorate the unity of the people and included the rainbow symbol plus the four native crests of Nishga society; the wolf, the eagle, the killer whale and the raven.

Bert McKay of Aiyansh talked with pride about the totem pole and the new school complex.

"This school that you see here didn't happen overnight. It's been a hundred years that we have been demanding equal opportunity, and today this is a dream of our forefather's coming true. Nishga will be taught in this school. Hunting, fishing, cooking by traditional means will also be taught. We know the value of using education to preserve our way of life and language."

184

A large expanse of lava rock covers twelve miles of the Nass valley. The presence of rich mineral deposits here is one reason the government is eager to get control of the land. But this is also sacred land to the Nishga. One day as we sat on this barren landscape Chief MacMillan described the volcanic eruption.

"Many years ago there was a river flowing down toward that mountain and, where we are sitting now there was a creek running into the main river. The young people began playing cruel games with the humpback salmon. They would cut strips of jackpine and light them like candles and push them into the backs of the salmon, then let go. The salmon would leap up the river and the kids would enjoy the sight. The old people warned the young that if they sent fire in this way up the river God would send fire back down. And he did. There was a rumbling noise and the mountain erupted."

Chief MacMillan said this story is told to all young children today as it has been for generations. It is told he says because it is the truth and because it teaches a respect for all of God's creatures.

The old people are greatly respected in Nishga life. Their advice is sought in every decision-making situation and their counsel, born of experience and wisdom, is followed.

Both young and old are united in their determination to keep their land. They would like the laws of British Columbia and Canada rewritten so that they might have enough control over their property to at least share in the decision concerning its future. They are not against the development of the minerals, lumber, fish and other riches of the valley. They simply want a say in how it is done.

The land claim problem was on everyone's mind, including Father John Blyth, Archdeacon of Caledonia diocese. Father Blyth was an adopted son of the Nishga. This was not just a formality. His adoption into the tribe was a very real thing. He was one of them.

I asked him, as a priest and as an adopted son, what were his hopes for the Nishgas.

"I have many hopes," he replied. "In regard to the land claims, I think it will take us a very long time to get them settled. It is very difficult for people from the outside to understand what the Nishga mean when they say the land is not for sale. A similar example would be the Israelites and the promised land. This land of the Nass Valley is Nishga holy land. It is given by God. We are stewards of it and are responsible for its development."

The church is very important to the people of Aiyansh. Emotionally and geographically it is the centre of the community. Everything seems to revolve around it and the band council office. Chief Hubert MacMillan has become a priest of the church; much of the service is conducted in the Nishga language. The vestments are made of the traditional button blankets and all appointments and art work reflect the Nishga culture.

"People here see no problem with the Christian faith," explained John Blyth, "because it has been indiginized. It is very much a part of the Nishga life."

The church looks after their spiritual needs, the river and the forests provide their food. But the land; this is the source of their deepest nourishment.

Many of the interviews we filmed were done in Aiyansh but for some we loaded a motor boat with our equipment and crossed the swollen Nass river to Old Aiyansh, now a deserted ghost town. The entire village was forced to move to its new site in 1968 after repeated flooding threatened its very life.

Some families return occasionally to smoke the salmon, tend a few gardens and just reminisce while walking through the beautiful old houses with their hand-hewn timbers. I was shown where white homesteaders had crossed the frozen river on snowmobiles during the winter, ransacked the homes and even stole pews from the magnificent old church.

Some of the interviews were conducted in the quiet groves of fir that surround Aiyansh. While the setting was superb we were constantly fighting the "no-seeums," a tiny species of blackfly. Daily my legs and arms became raw and swollen with thousands of bites. I held out as long as I could, but finally had to visit the nurses station for antibiotic shots and ointment.

The final day of our visit was marked by a community dinner of traditional Nishga food prepared for us at the home of Bert McKay. Young and old dropped in throughout the afternoon to say good-bye to the crew and to visit with their friends. The day passed in much laughter, eating, and singing. Everyone seemed reluctant to part, especially those of us who had to leave the valley and return to Vancouver and Toronto.

Long after our programme had been aired and after my "no-seeum" scars had disappeared, I recalled the warmth and sincerity with which the Nishgas talked of their community, their families, and above all, their land, which was not for sale, at any price.

Dorothy Day

PEOPLE THE LIGHT
SHINES THROUGH

Poverty horrified me so, made me so sick
at heart, that I became morbid about it.
I just had to live there myself.

Defining the term "saint" presents much the same problem as
defining "superstar." Who are they? Why are they so named?

I've never cared much for the traditional saints we read about
in church history, or see likenesses of in stained glass. They are
somehow frozen in a time long gone. It's difficult to imagine
them as real people. Often when you read their biographies you
wonder why they were ever canonized. It is perhaps best to view
them from a distance and let them live only as symbols of godliness. A little girl, whose only exposure to saints was seeing them
portrayed in the stained glass windows of her church was asked
by her priest, "What is a saint?" She answered, "They are people
the light shines through." That is likely as good a description
as we'll ever get, or need.

A definition for a modern saint presents an equally challenging
problem. These people are not formally canonized by the church,

but rather labelled by an enthusiastic media. Mother Teresa, Jean Vanier, Cardinal Leger, Anthony Bloom, Dorothy Day and many more have been described as "saints in our time." They reject the label and we do them an injustice by applying it to them. They are not merely symbols. They are living, working, people with a passion to serve, animated examples of that godliness.

I once discussed modern day "saints" with Francine du Plexis Gray, whose brilliant *New Yorker* articles chronicled the activities of the New Left during the 1960's. I asked her if any of the people she wrote about during this time, the political activists, the "divine dissenters" as she called them, qualified as saints.

She said, "I think we should differentiate between saints and heroes. There are times when people have great political charisma, like President Kennedy. After he was martyred we made a saint of him. While he achieved great things and exemplified the values of a particular society, so does Willy Mays and this makes them heroes. A saint goes beyond the values of his time. We need more Martin Luther Kings and Caesar Chavez's but we haven't seen enough of them beyond a particular time of crisis in our political history to tell if they are any more than heroes."

"Is there anyone?" I persisted.

"Yes, there is. I can think of one contemporary saint alive in the United States, one person who to me is clearly a saint, and that's Dorothy Day."

In the heart of New York's Bowery district Dorothy Day lives and works for the homeless and the hungry. Her famous open hospitality to the poor started in 1933 with the opening of St. Joseph's house. This was followed in later years by numerous other houses and farms for the poor and homeless. In 1933 she co-founded, with Peter Maurin, the *Catholic Worker* newspaper. Her literary credits climbed over the years. *On Pilgrimage, Loaves and Fishes, The Long Loneliness* are only a few of her many famous books. In England they call Dorothy Day "The Charles Dickens of America."

She is committed to total dedication, total liberation, total egalitarianism, and her commitment inspires others.

I met her in the summer of 1970. We talked in a small room overlooking the infamous Bowery district. This was at the height of the Vietnam War and though she was very involved in the anti-war movement and was considered quite a political force in the country, that day we talked of other things.

I asked her to tell me about the Bowery and she looked wistfully out of the window for a moment. "The Bowery is 3rd Avenue and it used to be a real bowery, a very beautiful country street in early New York. But now it's just a name. It's a name synonymous with skid row. In Chicago it's West Madison Street and it's some other street in some other city.

"It's made up of a whole bunch of small hotels where you used to be put up for 35¢ a night, but the cost now has gone up to $2.00 a night. You see everybody is profiteering. Inflation simply means get all you can. These places are paid for by welfare, but they are run by private concerns so the corruption seeps down to the owners of these flophouses. Everyone suffers because everyone is out to get what they can get. There is a great lack of any kind of housing for the destitute."

I asked her when her interest in the poor began.

"When I was fifteen, living in Chicago, the poverty in the stockyard area, the jungle we called it, made me interested in the whole social question. My father was a newspaperman working in Chicago so I went to the University of Illinois. I met a socialist there who had come from New York to speak and she told me about the work of the socialist party in New York and how some of their representatives in Albany were trying to do something about conditions on the east side. My father was a southerner with very definite views. He said no daughter of his was going to work and most certainly not work on a newspaper, which was what I wanted to do. So I left home and came to New York and got a job on a socialist newspaper.

"I'll never forget when I arrived in New York. I walked down the streets of the east side until I came to a tenement with a 'room for rent' sign. I walked up the smelliest flight of stairs you could imagine. It was a cold, damp place, full of the smells of stale cooking, but there I met the most wonderful Russian Jewish family. The parents couldn't speak any English, but the children could and they let me have a room that opened on the hall with one toilet for the whole floor.

"I went there to live because poverty horrified me so, made me so sick at heart, that I became morbid about it. I just had to live there myself, and you know, I grew to love it, not the poverty, but the people. I realized that you could be happy wherever you were because it's people that make for happiness, not surroundings.

"Look what people go through in wartime and they're able to take it. And in time of revolution, time of transition, people put up with all kinds of things. They're capable of far more than

189

we know.

"We actually started our work on 15th Street near First Avenue, but then a woman gave us the use of this house when the apartments became empty. Her uncle had built the place around 1850. We didn't have a soup line to begin with. It came later. What we did have was all this room so we provided a place to sleep. The men needed clothes so we gathered up old cast off clothing from around the neighbourhood. Sometimes all we could give them were newspapers to stuff inside their shirts since we had no overcoats. Sometimes all we could do was offer a cup of coffee. Then neighbours started bringing in leftover food. We began scrounging ingredients to make soup. I've seen a thousand men stretching in a line down the street, building bonfires in the gutters to keep warm in the wintertime, waiting for a bowl of soup. Our Italian neighbours had such a sense of hospitality they never once complained of having fires built in front of their homes."

I asked her, "Dorothy, I've talked to people, not only in North America but all over the world who refer to you as a saint, because of your many years of dedication to the poor. How do you feel about this?"

She answered, "I'm sure it must have been the Irish who told you this, because they call everyone a saint. You know, my sainted mother...my sainted aunt."

I assured her it wasn't just the Irish and wondered if the label embarrassed her.

"That kind of thing doesn't do our work any good. It gives the impression that it is not ordinary kind of work that ordinary people ought to be doing. Everyone ought to be doing it not just saints or special people. I don't regard it as a compliment at all. It makes you sound like a screwball living in a world of dreams. This is no dream world. We see things very clearly. We see poverty and hunger and loneliness. We see slum neighbourhoods being torn down and nothing put up for the poor. And we know it isn't necessary in a country like ours that people should have to live like this. The work we do is a protest against the system. We are a radical movement but it's considered safe because it's got religion attached to it. So instead of being called protestors which we are, we're called saints."

We talked for a while about active faith, putting ones beliefs and values into everyday action so as to cure the ills of society.

"Every time I look at the moon now I think if men, through their tremendous courage and their great mental capacity, can figure out how to go to the moon, think what could be accomplished if they developed their spiritual capacity to the same extent. But man seems to neglect that aspect of his being.

"People are searching for their spiritual force though. I think we are beginning to realize that man is not just body and mind. He is spirit and soul as well. People are now going in for transcendental meditation and Zen and back to the study of I Ching, looking for the sources of this thing that has so fascinated man: his spiritual capacities. Young people are searching for it. It's part of the reason they are now wandering around the country and wearing odd clothes and not cutting their hair. They want to be different. They are looking for something different. It is a search, a struggle for spiritual growth. And it is a very real thing."

After so many years of struggle and deprivation wasn't it time to pack it all in and take a rest from the daily, grinding misery?

"I've become very much at home here. I'm among friends. We operate in great difficulty but we keep going. We don't have the money to comply with all the regulations, the fire laws and the health laws, but we try. The firemen come once in awhile. They have to inspect every house. They go through our house and they see ten beds to a floor and they say 'who all lives here?' Well, I make up a little fiction. I say this is my house and these people are all my friends and they just laugh and let it go. They know what it's all about."

Dorothy Day at eighty-three continues to devote her life to others. Her fight for the downtrodden, the poor, the workers and the persecuted has been a lifelong commitment.

This same woman who defended anarchists Sacco and Vanzetti, the fish peddler and the shoemaker charged with murdering two payroll guards in 1920 and finally executed in 1927, also led protests against the Vietnam War in 1969. She marched with the dust bowl farmers in the 1930's and with Cesar Chavez.

Social justice is not a sometime thing with her. It is her whole life. She has been called "the greatest woman of our time," yet she doesn't have the high profile of a Mother Teresa or a Barbara Ward. For many years the media shied away from her. They found it difficult to "present" her. They couldn't bring themselves to write glowingly about a socialist who was a foe of capitalism and big government, had a prison record, defended lawbreakers, lived common-law, had an illegitimate child and published a newspaper which expounded the purest of Christian thought and action.

The fact remains that the light shining through Dorothy Day is clear and consistent. Of such stuff saints are surely made.

ON PRAYER

What constitutes prayer? Do prayers do any good? Can you change God's mind with prayer? Can you intercede for someone else by praying?

The question "Do you pray?" is not usually asked in television interviews, yet when it is posed it evokes very interesting and revealing answers. I have asked it often on *Man Alive* to people from all walks of life, and it invariably opens up an area of discussion that allows the viewer to see a deeper and more personal dimension to the guest.

What constitutes prayer? Do prayers do any good? Should you pray by rote or extemporaniously? Can you change God's mind with prayer? Can you intercede for someone else by praying?

Some of these questions are answered by people to whom prayer is a very important part of their lives and who I was lucky enough to interview on *Man Alive*.

Many people, when they meet Canada's Jean Vanier are aware of being in a kind of prayerful presence. He seems to radiate an aura of tranquility wherever he goes. His name has become synonomous with care and compassion for the mentally handicapped. *L'Arche* (the ark), a complex of group homes and sheltered workshops in Troisly-Breuil, France is headquarters for this son of Canada's late Governor General and his mother Madame Madeline Vanier. Similar homes have been set up to work with mentally retarded adults in several countries around the world.

During an interview with Jean, filmed on one of his return visits to Montreal, I asked him why people found it necessary to pray.

"Man has a vision of an unlimited world. He experiences dissatisfaction and frustration with his limited world. There is discord in the heart of man when he asks himself 'What eventually is reality? Is reality my car, and going to work, riding the Métro, my house, making money?' Occasionally there is a breakthrough, a discovery of what I call 'the source of life.'

"The man of prayer has a desire to enter in and touch the source of life, to know it and experience it. This desire comes from his incapacity to fit into a world that is too structured, too walled.

"Of course transcendental experience can be a flight from reality. We find this in occultism. People fly from reality into the unreality of the occult. You find it also in the drug world; a reach for some transcendental experience that has the taste of the eternal because it helps transcend time. You break through the barrier and are presented with a world that is outside of time.

"But at the heart of man is not always their flight from reality. It can also be a call which is very deep in one. A great search for the unlimited, a quest for knowledge, unlimited knowledge, a something in man which is always making him go forward. Man is not static.

"I believe that when we enter into the world of prayer God sends his spirit. The spirit of God draws us into the secret paths of prayer, the silence of prayer. The spirit of God teaches us to love; and you can't enter into the world of love without loving your brothers and your sisters. It's an opening up to other people; to their suffering, their joys, their peace. And this opening up of our beings, obviously is the world of prayer.

"It is necessary that my heart be open to all. If I close myself off from my brothers, this closing action makes me closed to God."

"We've been talking about individual prayers," I said. "What about group prayer?"

"Man is a very individual and unique being, a flower that no other flower is comparable to. Each one of us is like this. But, the strange thing is that we're also made for a bouquet. In a bouquet all the flowers harmonize. A man cannot do anything without his brothers. He doesn't appear on this world parachuted from some strange heaven, he flows out or erupts from the womb of his mother. He needs people. He needs to be nourished by people. He needs to be loved by people. From the moment he appears on the earth to the moment he leaves the earth, his life is a beautiful relationship with all sorts of people. These relationships can be opening or they can be closing, giving or taking. It is quite normal to pray together because we group and yearn together for collective needs, for our own needs and those of the world.

"Grouping together for prayer is important because we need this community and God manifests himself to us in this movement of love.

"Prayer is a movement from words to gradual silence. It is similar to other human conditions; the relationship between man and woman for example. A man and a woman will begin by talking. Then they enter a world where affection takes over. There's a communication of ideas and feelings. From that sharing comes union, the taking of the hand, the kiss. But this entering into the world of silent union begins with words. So it is with prayer. It is a union, and opening up of our being, not to something that is far away, but to someone who is very close to us and who loves us."

I asked how he felt about people who, when they pray, ask God for things, making him into a sort of celestial bellhop.

"This is a real defamation and abuse of prayer. We should ask God to give us peace or love and hope for the hopeless, but we shouldn't depend on God for the things we should do ourselves or for things just to flatter our egos; to pass an exam or to get a Buick for Christmas. Jesus says that if you remain in my love, whatever you ask for, you will receive, that is if you 'remain in my love.' So if the poor man turns to God and says, 'give us this day our daily bread' or the poor farmer who needs rain comes to God to ask for it, this is acknowledging God as a father. To ask him for something, as a child to his father, can be a very beautiful thing."

"How does Jean Vanier pray?"

"I would hope it is something along the line of what I have been saying. When I am in a state of nervousness, or in a trying situation, or very tired I feel a call to prayer because I have lost that peace. Something has gone wrong and I am becoming grieved. Perhaps it's the yearning of my own fatigue or inadequacies or sinfulness. I ask for forgiveness until I feel that touch of peace, an interior silence, which in a way is like an answer. There are other times frankly when my yearnings are not great enough and I simply fall asleep. My days are long and my activities manifold. They begin early and end late, but there would be very few days when I did not give quite a bit of time to prayer. They might be just short moments of yearning, but I try to stay in a state of prayer. Even when I talk to people, or listen to people, I try not to leave what I call the 'climate of prayer.'

"I'm not trying to push the aspect of prayer being useful to human activity, yet I find that men of action are men who pray. Dag Hammarskjold for example, and my father, and other people I know like them, spent a half hour or an hour each day just peacefully contemplating, quietly resting, yearning secretly for the spirit, the light and peace they carried in them. It provided a vision of man and a future of mankind that is much deeper than most; a sinking back to an eternal vision. I think a man of prayer will have this and be able to discover what is important in the things that are happening around him. He'll be able to decide. I think one of the fruits of prayer is discernment.

"Prayer can be a kind of therapy that brings equilibrium, peace, strength and internal force. One must not forget however, that prayer is essentially adoration and thanksgiving. It is the child asking the father, and thanking the father. It is the lover saying he loves and resting in the arms of his loved one. It is wonderment at beauty, the beauty of the father, the beauty of the loved one and the beauty of the universe that he has given us."

*   *   *

I interviewed Chief Dan George in the fall of 1979. His frail, slight body was confined to a wheel chair and his eighty years were taking their toll of his faculties, but his magnificent face, probably the most photogenic I have ever seen, still worked its magic on the television camera.

Near the end of our discussion I asked him if he prayed. His response became one of the most requested items in *Man Alive* history. Thousands have been printed and sent to viewers who heard his words that night and wanted a printed copy for them-selves.

"All tribes in North America used to say this prayer daily, even before Christopher Columbus came to our shore."

Oh, Great Spirit whose voice I hear in the wind, whose breath gives life to the world, hear me!

I come to you as one of your many children. I am small and weak. I need your strength and your wisdom.

May I walk in beauty. Make my eyes ever behold the red and purple sunset. Make my hands respect the things that you have made and my ears sharp to hear your voice.

Make me wise so that I may know the things that you have taught your children, the lessons you have hidden in every leaf and rock.

Make me strong, not to be superior to my brothers, but to be able to fight my greatest enemy — myself.

Make me ever ready to come to you with straight eyes, so that when my life fades, as the fading sunset, my spirit will come to you without shame.

*　　*　　*

A humourous incident related to prayer occurred in the fall of 1976 just prior to the United States election when *Man Alive* did a programme on candidate Jimmy Carter. We travelled to Plains, Georgia and talked with neighbours and relatives of Carter to try and find out what kind of a person this born again peanut farmer was. At the recently held Democratic National Convention, Carter had been highly praised by Martin Luther King Sr. So we decided to stop off in Atlanta to talk to this venerable old Baptist preacher and the father of the great civil rights leader.

In the hot Georgia sun, seated near the simple but beautiful memorial to his martyred son, King was the picture of Christian benevolence and charity until we got on the subject of prayer.

"Do you pray for Jimmy Carter?" I asked.

"Oh yes, daily."

"Do you pray for Gerald Ford?"

"I pray for everybody, but I ain't going to ask God to bless Gerald Ford."

"Why not? He's the President," I insisted.

"I ain't going to ask God's blessing on a man so's he can keep on doing the wrong thing," was his reply.

There was another prayer on *Man Alive* that prompted viewers by the hundreds to respond with requests for copies. A young Winnipeg girl, terminally ill with cancer, told us she read this prayer over and over to give her courage in the face of her tragedy. She didn't know who had written it and our researchers couldn't find the author either. It became known simply as Joscelyn's prayer.

One night, a man had a dream.
He dreamed he was walking along the beach
with the Lord.
Across the sky flashed scenes from his life.
For each scene he noticed two sets of footprints in the sand
one belonging to him — the other to the Lord.
When the last scene of his life flashed before him,
he looked back at the footprints in the sand,
and he noticed that many times along the path of his life
there was only one set of footprints.
He also noticed that it happened
at the very lowest and saddest times in his life.
This really bothered him and he questioned the Lord about it.
"Lord, you said that once I decided to follow you,
you'd walk with me all the way.
But I've noticed that during the most difficult times in my life,
there is only one set of footprints.
I don't understand why in times when I needed you most,
You would leave me."
The Lord replied:
"My precious, precious child,
I love you and I would never, never leave you
during your trials and suffering.
When you see only one set of footprints,
it was then that I carried you!"

* * *

In a programme devoted entirely to the subject of prayer I interviewed Brother David Steindl-Rast, a Benedictine monk, who is also a Doctor of Psychiatry and student of Zen. Viennese born, he took his monastic vows in 1953 and is Hermit-in-Residence at the Benedictine Grange near West Redding, Connecticut.

Brother David called prayer "the lifting up of heart and mind to God. It can be something very simple. Something that gives

197

you a lift. You're driving along on the highway and from the car in front of you children are looking out of the back window, perhaps making faces at you, and it lifts your heart. It lifts it up to God and as long as we don't deliberately hold it back, that is a moment of prayer in the deepest sense.

"Prayer is concentration, but not in the sense of shutting everything out. It is the kind of concentration that actually widens our field and that widening might be called wonderment. A child does everything prayerfully. When you watch a small child he is perfectly concentrated, so much so you can hardly distract him; not with the narrowmindedness like a scientist watching an experiment, but with the wonderment of an artist or of a mystic.

"The one word I would use to characterize prayer is gratitude. Living life gratefully is not taking things for granted. When you take things for granted you go through a life where nothing is meaningful to you. You should stop and consider the given reality even though it may not always be the kind of gift that you really want — it's a gift, and the only appropriate response to a gift is 'thank you.' This takes a lot of faith and courage and trust and hope and love, but when you get yourself to that kind of inner acceptance, then you are truly grateful.

"It seems to me we should take the whole reality of prayer out of the strictly religious context and religious vocabulary and speak for a while about 'grateful living.' If we cultivate those moments in our daily life when we are filled with gratefulness and those times when we can act gratefully, then we are putting prayer on a kind of human level, which in many ways is a much deeper religious context.

"If you look around among your acquaintances you'll find that the grateful people are the happy ones. This means that we hold the very key to our happiness because when we are grateful we are saying what I call 'the great yes to life.' You can't be grateful without saying yes, and that yes puts you in tune with everything including yourself. Gratefulness always comes from the heart. You can't be half-heartedly grateful. When it comes from the heart this is the very 'spot' of prayer and the very 'spot of communication with God.' It is the 'spot' where we are together. People nowadays say, 'that person really has it all together.' That means he lives from the heart and is in communion with God, and with others. It's the opposite of being alienated and it makes us very happy.

"All of our life can be more prayerful if we give as well as take. Life is give and take. To be fully alive one must give and take, but we seem to have lost to a great extent the capacity to give ourselves. We only grab, grope and take. This becomes quite clear in the way we express ourselves. We constantly say I take a cup of coffee. I take a break. I take a meal. I take a walk. I take a shower. I take, take, take, all day long. It all adds up to taking life and when we take life, we kill it.

"What we have to learn is that every time we take we also give ourselves. A cup of coffee first thing in the morning can be a prayer of gratitude if we give ourselves to it, instead of just taking."

I questioned Brother David about request prayers where people ask for things from God.

"I think it is fair to say that for most people prayer and prayer petition are identical. We might question the why of prayer petition. If God is almighty and good and gives us all the things we need anyway, why would God even want us to ask for anything? This ties in again with thanksgiving and gratefulness. You could ask why does a mother hold the cookie out to the child and says 'say please' and won't give it unless the child says 'please?' Is it that the mother wants to show her power over the child by withholding it? No, the mother wants to make the child grateful. If the child learns to say please then it will be grateful when he gets the cookie and will not simply take it for granted. The whole idea of prayer petition is to foster gratefulness, because if we just take God's gifts for granted then we will not be happy with them."

I asked him about the kind of praying that is intended to save the life of a dying friend. Is this not trying to change God's mind?

"No. We are not changing God's mind simply because the mind of God is not made up yet and you can't change a mind that's not made up. We should look at it this way. We cannot pray except in God and this is true for all religions. It is the Holy Spirit praying in us and the Holy Spirit is God. So it is God praying in us and that is why prayers are always answered. They may not be answered exactly the way we thought, but that is because we didn't understand what the Holy Spirit within us was really saying.

"If I had to say anything to parents it would be to encourage them to teach their children prayers, beautiful prayers to help them realize life's gifts, to be in touch with God and to experience the joy that comes from being grateful."

ON HOPE

*A continuing uplifting emphasis, a strong
theme of optimism, a feeling that it is possible
to change a situation, a sense of hope.*

In an introduction at a convention where I was to be the after dinner speaker, the master of ceremonies ended his remarks by exclaiming, "...and now I give you, that happy troubadour of the Canadian spirit, Roy Bonisteel."

Not being used to such a flashy introduction I was somewhat embarrassed, but also puzzled. After being involved with programmes on poverty, loneliness, famine, torture, child abuse, death and dying, I was surprised to be called a "happy troubadour." When I thought about this later, however, it seemed that with the majority of *Man Alive* programmes, there was a continuing uplifting emphasis, a strong theme of optimism, a feeling that it is possible to change a situation, a sense of hope.

The two people I have briefly noted here helped to give that positive quality to *Man Alive*, to me, and through me to millions of viewers.

We approached Dr. Bruno Bettleheim, the American child-psychoanalyst, when *Man Alive* was preparing a programme on prejudice. He agreed to talk to us about the subject and the interview was arranged for the fall of 1977 in Chicago. Vienna born, Bettleheim has become internationally known through his best selling books in the field of social psychology and his work with emotionally disturbed children.

As often happens in interviews, the conversation covered a much wider area than our assigned topic, and we found ourselves with enough material for another programme. Using fantasy and children's fairy tales as symbols, Bettleheim talked about hope and meaning in modern life. His remarks were much appreciated by parents who were searching for ways to instill in their children a positive approach to life.

"We all need help coping with the problems of life. Look at all the successful books telling people how to cope. Look at all the efforts to deal with the difficulties of living. The encounter groups, the spread of Oriental religions, shows that people are looking for something beyond the immediate present and the harsh reality in which we all live our lives. I think we all have a need for, I hesitate to say something higher, something more meaningful. I think there's a great drought in the life of many people because life has become meaningless to them. It's not that they don't struggle very hard, but that they wonder what it's all about. I think we all need meaning in life.

"Typically, many fairy stories such as Hanzel and Gretel, Snow White and many others are about people lost in the forest, not knowing which way to turn. These are very ancient symbols of man in crisis, developmental crisis, mental crisis, emotional crisis and moral crisis of being lost, and not knowing which way to turn. These are the same developmental crises we all go through as we move out of childhood into adolescence, out of adolescence into maturity and speaking of my own age, out of maturity into old age.

Before Snow White is kicked out by her stepmother she didn't work. She didn't do anything. She just had a jolly good time. Then comes the crisis. She is lost in the forest. Out of the court of her stepmother she is lost in an entirely different work-a-day world of the dwarfs. Then she meets the temptation of the Queen. And she falls for it.

"The last temptation is the apple with which we are all familiar from the biblical story of paradise, the snake and Adam and Eve, which, by the way, is also a fairy story of temptation. Still we see that a solution is possible despite this. A bright future is possible no matter what befalls us.

"Take the story of Cinderella, for example. It is very old. It was written down for the first time in AD 700 in China. The Chinese origin can still be recognized from Cinderella's extremely tiny foot which was a sign of beauty and virtue in China. But what I like about Cinderella is this. After she goes to the ball in her beautiful clothes and the prince falls in love with her, the story could end there. But it doesn't. She runs away. Three times as a matter of fact. The prince has to come and see her in her dejected state, in her dirty rags. Because, the story tells us that it wouldn't be a happy life, it wouldn't be right, if the prince would select her only for her good looks and for her beautiful clothes and jewelry. So Cinderella tells us by implication that you have to be chosen for the person you are, not outward appearances.

"But the greatest value of the fairy tale is that it gives hope because even fairy tale heroes feel persecuted. Cinderella feels persecuted by the step mother and her evil sisters. But the difference is that while Cinderella is persecuted there is always hope in her. She never gives up hope and because she never gives up hope, she is rescued.

"I work with psychotic children. One very bright and sensitive psychotic child I worked with got well and afterwards was reflecting on what makes good parents. How could parents prevent children from becoming insane as she did? And this is what she told me.

" 'A good parent hopes for you. My parents never hoped for me.'

"I think the fairy story instills this hope in the child. It tells us that a happy ending is available if you struggle hard enough, if you don't give up, if you live virtuously and do the right thing."

Given the size and complexity of many world problems today it is hard to believe that one person can effect change. The "what can one person do" syndrome is understandable. Daily media coverage of world crises of incredible enormity leave us reeling with helplessness.

I have encountered many people on *Man Alive* who single handedly tackle world problems with considerable success.

One example is Father Murray Abraham, a Canadian whose whole life takes the form of an unswerving conviction that "something has to be done and I can make a difference."

Murray Abraham grew up in Nova Scotia. At fifteen he was

the youngest person to enter the Jesuit training programme. After seven years he was sent to the Canadian Jesuit mission in Darjeeling, India. He was ordained in 1954 and was sent to St. Alphonsus School in Kurseong in North Eastern India, as headmaster.

"While I was teaching one day the wall of the school caved in. Clearly something had to be done to replace the buildings. The poverty of the area was abysmal. Learning was impossible as the children would pass out from hunger in front of my eyes. The Indian government provided only partial assistance for education up to Grade Four and then nothing, so many families couldn't afford to send their children to school. The Bengali government also decided one day that no one could be principal of a high school without a Masters degree in education, so I returned to Canada."

He spent a year at St. Mary's in Halifax picking up an M.A. and a great deal more. While there he launched his first "pilgrimage" for St. Alphonsus. The Bishop of Halifax gave permission for Father Murray to enlist fifty "friends" who would send about four dollars per month to his school. Needing more, Murray went to see the Bishop of Moncton who also agreed to fifty. Encouraged, Murray struck out across Canada in an old Volkswagon lining up more support. Each "friend" was to give up dessert once a week and send the cost of the dessert to him. The contributor was to sign a Book of Life, thereby making a commitment to help the less fortunate. The commitment on the part of many Canadians and the reminder once a week of what they were doing when dessert was skipped, was as important to Father Abraham as the money.

Back in Kurseong the enterprising headmaster and his students literally dug in to build a new school. Rock was chiselled out of the Himalayan mountain sides, then smashed with hammers to provide the aggregate for cement blocks. Sand and water were carried by hand. The Indo-China war and ensuing inflation pushed the cost of a bag of cement from six dollars and fifty cents to twenty-three dollars. Money was scarce. The hunger-weakened students could work only one hour a day. It took seven years to erect the building.

In 1968, ulcers, stress and a seventy-five thousand dollar debt accompanied Father Abraham into the Foothills Hospital in Western Canada. Three months later, his health on the mend, he launched another cross country tour. This time his goal was to feed his starving students and the people in the community.

Another Book of Life, more missed desserts, and by late 1969 he was back at St. Alphonsus.

He set up a poultry business on the roof of the school in order to provide at least one egg a day for each of his students. This eventually grew into a poultry business of six thousand five hundred hens. Eggs were sold throughout the community and profits were used to buy pigs, cattle, and seed for adjoining land. Canadian agriculturist Malcolm Davidson visited St. Alphonsus to advise on crop varieties, fertilizer and modern farming techniques. Land that never knew a blade of grass flourished with corn, soy beans and pasture. Truckloads of produce, eggs, meat, vegetables and cut flowers were sold to the hotels in Darjeeling.

The building programme never really stopped. Barns, roads and retaining walls were added by the now increased enrolment of 1480 students, who were able to put their academic studies immediately to practical use in construction, business practice, animal husbandry, agricultural science, commerce and numerous other endeavours.

I caught up with Father Abraham in Ottawa when he returned to Canada for another visit to make new "friends." This time the project was a graduate school, an agricultural college. After two years at the college the students will have the opportunity to start farming on their own, small plots of land being provided by the Indian government on a co-operative basis.

The Father Abraham story is a remarkable one: a Roman Catholic priest devoting his life to caring for Hindus; a teacher whose pupils learn self-sufficiency and pride in their accomplishments; a man who saw a need and responded through his own humanity and the humanity he encouraged in others.

What can one person do? I commented to Father Abraham that after all Kurseong was only one community in a country of six hundred million. Certainly it was a success story in the fight against poverty and ignorance, but wasn't it just a drop in the bucket?

He answered. "That's true. But everything starts as a drop in the bucket. Jesus Christ was born in a stable in Bethlehem. Who would have thought that was going to transform the world? Think of the few pioneers who came to settle in Western Canada. Look at the country now. Somebody has to begin. Ghandi was only one man. I remember when Mother Teresa began in Calcutta. She was only one. It makes sense to look at where you are, at the situation you are in and ask yourself, how can I change it? I don't think we do that enough!"

THE SELLING
OF CHRIST

*It was only a matter of time before the
religion huckster realized he could package
and sell Christ as profitably as a laundry
detergent and as unashamedly as religious
indulgences were sold of old.*

In 1922 an enterprising New York real estate company paid to
have some property mentioned on the regular transmissions of a
fledgling local radio station and became the first commercial
advertiser in broadcasting. Millions of commercials and billions
of dollars worth of air time later, broadcasting, particularly television, became the most powerful advertising vehicle yet devised.
The advertiser had achieved his ultimate goal, a persuasive and
persistent salesman actually invited into the living room of the
customer where his wares could be enticingly displayed before a
captive and somewhat mesmerized customer.

The subtle and manipulative power of television commercials
is awesome and it was only a matter of time before the religion
huckster realized he could package and sell Christ as profitably
as a laundry detergent and as unashamedly as religious indulgences were sold of old.

Currently running on stations all over North America, for example, is a series of one minute spots soliciting money for the PTL club. The initials of this North Carolina based organization, headed by evangelist Jim Bakker, alternately stand for Praise The Lord and People That Love. Some observers claim it should be tagged Pass The Loot. One of their advertisements shows an elderly and somewhat infirm woman concluding a telephone call with her children who apparently are not coming for an expected visit. She tearfully hangs up the phone, heads for her rocking chair and the remote control for her television set. As the image of Bakker comes on the screen, accompanied by a musical swell of violins, an announcer informs us that Grandma Nelson finds it hard to continue since Granpa Nelson went to "meet the Lord" last year. But if we send money to Jim Bakker this Grandma, and all the other Grandma Nelsons, will find the strength to carry on.

A second extremely well produced commercial portrays a distressed young woman with a handful of pills and a bottle of liquor preparing to commit suicide. Through a series of cuts we glimpse the PTL control room, the video tapes, monitors and cameras interspersed with shots of the pills, the bottle and tear-filled eyes. As Jim Bakker appears on the woman's television screen asking "Do you feel like life is not worth living?" she puts down the bottle, throws away the pills and relaxes into her chair with a smile. The announcer then urges us to send fifteen dollars a month to Jim Bakker.

Bakker also peddles prints of Jesus in various poses, one per month at one hundred dollars a picture. On a recent show Bakker even offered to sell kittens, newly born from his family cats, for one hundred thousand dollars. He said he was being facetious, but that if anyone wanted to send the money he would certainly accept it.

The basic format of the PTL club is that of a television talk show with a heavy accent on celebrities who witness to their conversion. It operates on a budget of over two million dollars a month and claims to have the largest single television studio in North America. Having the biggest operation, or the most stations, or the highest ratings or the most successful converts as guests, is very important to the television evangelist. There is constant jockeying for the lead, and depending what yardstick is used for measuring, positions constantly change in this religious race.

For several years Oral Roberts of Tulsa, Oklahoma held the

top spot with the largest syndicated religious programme in the world. When his televised healing sessions became less popular Roberts opted for star-studded prime time specials. His presidency of Oral Roberts University demanded much of his time and his son Richard took on more of the preaching duties.

This left the lead open for Rex Humbard and his *Cathedral of Tomorrow* broadcasts from Akron, Ohio. Humbard's business empire expanded as his heavy exposure brought increased donations.

Besides his five thousand seat Cathedral, built at a cost of $3,400,000, Humbard's Cathedral Enterprises Incorporated at one time owned an advertising agency, an electronics firm, a printing company, Mackinac College in Northern Michigan, a twenty-four story office tower in downtown Akron, an apartment building, a restaurant and the Real Form Girdle Company of Brooklyn, New York. His conglomerate began falling apart in the early seventies. Profits from the girdle company fell off. "Pantyhose killed us," said Humbard. His college only attracted one hundred and fifty students. They had anticipated an enrolment of seven hundred. The big blow fell however, when officials in six states banned the sale of Cathedral Securities because they were not properly registered. The United States Securities and Exchange Commission also asked a federal court to appoint a receiver to take over all Cathedral Enterprises' assets. According to the Securities and Exchange Commission the church had spent $7.3 million more than it had taken in over a period of eighteen months ending December 1972 and had $4.2 million more in liabilities than assets. Humbard reasoned that the government should allow him to count as assets fourteen million dollars that the church stood to inherit from people who had written the church into their wills. He managed to survive, partly through desperate pleas to his television faithful. Letters from Rex, his family members, and celebrities such as singing star Pat Boone, regularly flowed to the millions of names on his mailing list pleading for increased donations to save his ministry. He was forced to trim his operations to a more modest scale and his hold on the top rung of the religious TV ladder was relinquished.

There were plenty more waiting to take his place. Ernest Angley, and his Angel Productions also from Akron, who claims to heal in Christ's name with a blow to the forehead, Jimmy Swaggart from Baton Rouge, Louisiana, who croons and plays the piano between sermons; Texan James Robison and his "Wake Up America" campaign, Robert Schuller of California with his

Hour of Power positive thinking philosophy and Jerry Falwell of Lynchburg, Virginia who most observers would agree has now surpassed even Humbard at his peak. His syndicated *Old Time Gospel Hour* programmes cost more to produce per week than many top network shows. He spends five thousand dollars a minute or three hundred thousand dollars a week for air time. His yearly operating budget is fifty-six million dollars and for this he claims to reach twenty million viewers in North America and the Caribbean. His Liberty Baptist College, which he describes as a boot camp for evangelists, has a twenty-five hundred student enrolment which he is forcasting will grow to fifty thousand by the year 2000.

The old charge of "sheep stealing," which is levelled against most evangelists by mainline denominations, causes no worries for Falwell. "It's not a bad idea if people are being taken away from the liberal churches and put into Christ-oriented churches. When people write me I tell them to switch to a Bible believing church." He is very heavily involved with the political scene often speaking out against SALT II and other agreements the United States is attempting to negotiate with "Godless communist countries." He has formed "Moral Majority" a lobbying organization to pressure government officials into following his brand of democracy and free enterprise. "I'll get out of the political business when the politicians get out of all business," he says, and adds "We have an obligation to our children and our children's children to straighten this country out morally before she goes down the tubes."

His sentiments are echoed by Pat Robertson of *The 700 Club*. His Christian Broadcasting Network extends over two hundred stations. His upbeat, talk show format programme is undoubtedly the most sophisticated of its kind on the air. He is the son of a former United States Senator and himself a Yale Law School graduate, who speaks out regularly on behalf of conservative American politics. His newsletters regularly backed Ronald Reagan for president in the last election and said that government has no right to get involved with religious matters, such as prayer in school, abortion or the Equal Rights Amendment.

One of the most controversial broadcast evangelists is Herbert W. Armstrong whose World Wide Church of God embraces one hundred thousand members and collects over eighty million dollars annually. The operation is based in Pasadena. The State of California, after a lengthy battle, has finally received a ruling from the United States Supreme Court to allow its investigation of the church's financial structure. The State alleges misuse of the church's money through a siphoning off of contributions by Armstrong and his staff for personal use. The charges originated with some of the church's own members. Other members staunchly defend their elderly leader claiming "to investigate Herbert W. Armstrong is as though the State of California were questioning the integrity of Christ."

Equally well known to religious radio and television audiences is Herbert's son Garner Ted Armstrong who is now broadcasting his own syndicated programme after being cast out by his father for his "wordly behaviour."

Garner Ted says the free spending, power hungry organizations are giving evangelism a bad name and refers to shady deals and money squandering in his father's organization. The church offered him a fifty thousand dollar a year allowance to "keep his bad mouth shut," which he refused.

The reason for the church's incredible wealth is Herbert W. Armstrong's insistence that church members tithe, that is give ten per cent of their annual gross income. He bases this on his interpretation of the biblical injunction of Moses that man should "tithe his crop and his herds to the Lord." On top of this he demands a second and sometimes a third tithe as length of membership increases, plus special appeals for specific projects during the year. A loyal church member can end up giving one-third of his income annually to the church.

Money is the key factor that keeps the electronic church thriving. The purchase of air time alone, in the United States and Canada, amounts to over five hundred million dollars annually. This makes religion one of the top ten spenders in television advertising, in the company of Proctor and Gamble and General Motors. This revenue accounts for the broadcasting industry being loathe to take any steps to restrict the growth of these programmes.

In the United States, at last count, there were sixty syndicated religious television series. About half of these are, at various times, carried on Canadian stations. Most of the others are available to Canadian viewers from American border stations and they constantly plead for Canadian funds. Research shows that Canadian audiences are more generous than their American neighbours, sending twice as much money per viewer to keep their favourite evangelist in business.

For many years television evangelists didn't actually mention money in their request for support. They referred to "prayer offerings" or "love gifts." Now any pretense of delicacy has been abandoned and, not only are viewers urged to send money, but in many cases are told how much to send. However it is the mailing list that ranks with Holy Writ in the television ministry business. Names, addresses and postal codes are fed into computers as fast as they can be collected by offering books, records, pictures or religious trinkets over the air and by promoting toll-free numbers for viewers to call for prayer and counselling. The real pressure for support is then conducted through the mails as banks of automated typewriters spew out "personal" letters and pamphlets from the evangelist begging for dollars to keep the ministry thriving. Some letters are folksy and full of news about the evangelist's family and personal life. Others are strictly business, giving advice on how to borrow money from banks and loan companies or advice on arranging mortgages in order to get extra money to send. Some contain blank wills to be filled out with the evangelist's organization as beneficiary.

Canadians have sent me many copies of letters they have received as a result of getting on the mailing list of American evangelists. Many letters give the impression you are actually sending the money to God and that if he doesn't get it immediately Satan will take over the world.

Others use collection agency tactics, pointing out that the money was promised and that the evangelist won't be responsible if God sees fit to punish the tardy giver. Once on the mailing list not even death can ease the onslaught of petitions. One man sent me copies of letters still asking for money from his mother who had been dead for five years.

It is not difficult to understand why the financial harvest is so abundant. There are many who believe what the evangelist so persuasively says and honestly feel they are helping spread Christianity by sending donations. Millions of others are lonely and troubled and consider the evangelist a family member who comes in each day for a visit. It is hard to resist a charismatic celebrity who looks directly at you from your television set and says. "I love you. I care for you. I want to help you." When the next line is "send me some money," most viewers do.

For years, on television and radio, Billy Graham reigned supreme and carried with him considerable respect and admiration from his audience and from the mainline churches. He is a gifted orator and his theology, though conservative, is well presented. His credentials are valid. Only when local clergy realized that Graham was not so much saving lost souls as simply stirring up the already converted did their support wane. Graham, who demands that a high percentage of a city's clergy guarantee support for his crusade, found himself less and less in demand and began planning crusades in England, Australia, Korea and cutting back on his North American television specials. As one Montreal minister told me, "Graham takes over a city for a few days. He preaches to the people of my congregation who are already church goers. Then he packs up and leaves. And when these people want help with their problems, need counselling or visiting when they are sick or need someone to marry or bury them, they can't go to Billy Graham. He's long gone."

Personally I have always liked Billy Graham. I believe he's a sincere and honest man. I admire his dramatic preaching style, his ability to speak directly to issues and more importantly I have never thought he was trying to con or fleece his followers. I will, however, always remember an incident during Canada's centennial year when *Man Alive* covered the Billy Graham crusade in Toronto. On the last night of the event after an impassioned plea by Graham to come forward to the altar for personal redemption and commitment a stream of people made their way crying, singing and praying down the aisles. Our reporters were interviewing several people at this moment getting reactions to the crusade. We asked one man for his impressions of the evening.

"It has just been wonderful," he said. "It is without a doubt the most important event in my life."

"Are you going forward now to make your commitment?"

"Well, I'd like to," he answered, "but if I take the time to do that I'll miss my bus to Hamilton."

Graham of course is not without his critics. Many years later referring to this 1967 crusade, Reverend Clarke MacDonald, Secretary of the Board of Evangelism and Social Service for the United Church of Canada, was quoted as saying, "The tragedy is that the one who has done more to popularize the concept of evangelism than anyone else, has also sometimes by wooden interpretation of the Bible, by ultra simplistic answers to complex questions and by a too easy identification of the American way of life with the Kingdom of God, brought evangelism into disrepute in the minds of some. I listened as Billy Graham addressed forty thousand people in the Canadian National Exhibition Stadium some six years ago. After a vivid description of the deplorable moral and political state of the world he said, 'The United Nations can do nothing about it. Washington, Moscow, London and Ottawa can do nothing about it. Jesus Christ did it all two thousand years ago on the cross.' Such heady rhetoric, if taken seriously, renders earthly rulers impotent.''

For years Graham disassociated himself with politics and is on record as soundly criticizing fellow evangelist Bill Bright for trying to organize Evangelicals into a political bloc, but then he himself became closely associated with President Richard Nixon's White House. Many sensed that he had become Nixon's private chaplain and even during the Watergate episode Graham staunchily defended his president. It wasn't until transcripts of the oval office conversations were released, showing the expletive filled statements of cunning and conniving, that Graham finally and publicly criticized Nixon. By then the damage was done and Graham's image became somewhat tarnished through his association with a man who became a national disgrace.

The political arena has always been a powerful magnet for evangelical leaders, not by standing for office, but through pressure tactics on followers, organizations and elected representatives. One of the best examples is William Rohl Bright.

At thirty he was running a food business called Bright's California Confections and taking seminary courses at night when he had a ''vision'' in which God spoke to him and ''showed me the whole world and gave me the confidence that He would use me and others in this generation to reach the multitudes of the world.'' Figuring a generation to be about twenty-five years or so Bright reasoned he should evangelize the United States by the end of 1976 and convert the entire world by 1980. He began his work at the University of California at Los Angeles, winning over athletes, student leaders and political activists. With the slogan, ''Today the campus. Tomorrow the World'' he spread his Campus Crusade for Christ to over four hundred universities in the United States.

Bright's version of Christianity is simple. He calls it the Four Spiritual Laws: 1. God loves you and offers a wonderful plan for your life. 2. Man is sinful and separated from God, so he doesn't know about Law number 1. 3. Jesus Christ is God's only provision for man's sin. 4. We must individually receive Jesus Christ as Saviour and Lord, then we can know and experience God's love and plan for our lives.

In order to spread these laws and meet the deadlines which he felt God had ordained, Bright launched one of the most powerful and sophisticated marketing blitzes ever released on the unsuspecting public. Based in Atlanta, Bright's ''Here's Life'' campaign hit over two hundred cities in the United States and Canada in 1976 reaching a total of sixty million households. It was an advertising venture of gigantic proportions. Instead of promoting a new brand of toothpaste they were introducing and packaging Christ. "I found It" was declared on television, radio and in newspaper ads. Prime time television specials featuring show business celebrities, beauty queens and sports figures drove the message home. Bumper stickers and billboards carried the "I found It" teaser across North America, the Orient, Europe and South America. The operation was run on the same merchandising principles as a fried chicken franchise with local people being supplied with all the pre-tested marketing tools, computer print-outs, strategy booklets, training manuals and telephone follow-up techniques. In Chicago team members manned one hundred telephones fifteen hours a day. Over four hundred thousand volunteers joined the six thousand Campus Crusade staff to spread the gospel according to Bill Bright.

At the height of the campaign I talked with Bill Bright at his headquarters, a one-time resort hotel, high in the mountains overlooking San Bernadino, California. Besides running his thirty-four million dollars a year operation from here the hotel provides staff training and, at various times throughout the year, executive seminars are held to, according to Bright, "evangelize the wealthy." We stood on his spacious, rolling lawn at the edge of a massive swimming pool where Bright proudly announced he had baptized former Black Panther Eldridge Cleaver the year before. I asked him what he was really trying to do.

"We are trying and expecting to raise over a billion dollars for the glory of God to help send the gospel to the whole world."

"You really expect this?"

"Well, you see, if the God whom we worship is truly God, and He is, and if He is the creator of a hundred billion known galaxies, which astronomers tell us they know for sure exist, and if He so loved the world He gave His only begotten Son, and the scriptures say He's not willing that any soul perish but all should come repentent, then, I believe God will give us the ability to do this."

"What if it doesn't work out?"

"Our goal is to be expendable for Christ. Like the Kamikaze pilot of the Japanese air force we are willing to live and die for Christ if need be."

I didn't remind him that the Kamikaze pilots did not die for Christ, but I did ask about his emergence on the political scene.

I had been to Washington D.C. to see Bright's Christian Embassy. He had purchased a French style mansion from the Catholic Archdiocese, which called it "unfittingly grandiose," for five hundred thousand dollars donated by wealthy laymen. Several days each month Bright works out of the embassy in a low key attempt to promote Christian principles in government. In the born again atmosphere of the Carter administration, he found eager friends among senators, congressmen and other high ranking government officials.

"I am involved in government," he said, "because Jesus said we're to be the salt of the earth and the light of the world. The believer should bring the morality and spiritual influence of Christ into government, medicine, education, the professions and business. Every facet of life should be influenced by Christ."

When interviewing evangelists you become accustomed to their answering questions with Bible quotations. For some it is a defence mechanism that slips easily into their vocabulary when trying to avoid a direct answer. For many it is a speech pattern that has become habitual and is as natural for them as swearing is to some people.

Bill Bright, however, tends to use chapter and verse to back up facts and figures with no basis in accuracy.

"In 1962," he told me, "the highest court in the land, the Supreme Court, declared there's no place for God in the schools. The Bible and prayer were outlawed. An avalanche of evil came upon our country immediately following that decision, which was an official act of our highest court. Crime accelerated three hundred per cent through the next few years. We had the drug culture, the revolution that swept our nation, the bombing and burning of university buildings, the war in Vietnam and the disgrace of Watergate.

"God let us see ourselves as we really were, impotent, frustrated, confused people. And it was at that time, that the promise of God became very real to many millions of Christians. 'If my people who are called by my name will humble themselves and pray and seek my face and turn from their wicked ways, then will I hear from Heaven, forgive their sins, and heal their land.' "

Bright insisted that since the Campus Crusade for Christ started and the Here's Life campaign got into full swing crime had declined all over the nation.

I said it was my opinion that crime had been increasing in North America for many diverse reasons long before the Supreme

Court decision on prayer in school and that it was still on the increase according to police departments and social scientists. Bright had no intention of considering this and branded any other opinion as anti-Christian.

"I don't object to athiests saying that. Let the athiests speak. You know they don't have anything to say that one would listen to if people only have the chance to hear the truth. Jesus said, 'I am the way, the truth and the light!' The scripture says 'Ye shall know the truth and the truth shall set you free.' You see, Christ is truth.''

There is very little real dialogue possible with Bill Bright. He simply does not want to hear an opinion or idea that conflicts with his own. This is the source of much criticism by leading American theologians like Reverend Martin Marty. Marty, a Lutheran, is Associate Editor of the *Christian Century*, a professor at the University of Chicago and one of America's leading religious historians.

Commenting on Bright's mission he told me, "They are a menace to society to the degree that they succeed. They seem to say we're here to save all the other people and we don't know what the other people are here for. If you are not a believer, or not a Christian or if you're not their kind of Christian, they're interested in you only as a potential convert. They are all so cock sure there's never any room for doubt. If you resist or turn away, you're dismissed. Their computer systems, billboards, telephone soliciting, tracts being shoved under your nose constantly, are destructive to the image the world has of the hard working pastor quietly going about his or her business late at night comforting the lonely, or counselling the alcoholic who is fighting a Christian battle. They are a menace to other forms of Christian witness and other forms of evangelicalism. The history of North American revivals of the 'Here's Life' type usually show that the public builds up very defensive reactions against every other form of Christian presentation after such a hard sell.''

It's this hard sell that eventually brings the downfall of crusades such as this. Like any commercial saturation campaign the buyer's enthusiasm fades once the ads begin to bore, the bumper stickers start to peel and the warranty wears off. No matter how much money is spent to sway the public, no product can live up to the bloated claims of the promoter when it is misrepresented at the outset.

I believe some television evangelists start out sincerely believing they are called to preach the gospel to a wider parish and see the medium of television as a means of fulfilling that mission. When they discover they have tapped a vein of gold far richer than any offering plate could yield, the ministry becomes a business and instead of supporting and nourishing the viewer, the viewer supports them.

The *Cathedral of Tomorrow* broadcast for example began in a tent and served a small congregation of local believers. It became the success story of television evangelism and the model for others who envied that success.

The first time I met Rex Humbard was in September 1972 when *Man Alive* arranged for me to interview him and members of his organization on location in Cuyahoga Falls, a suburb of Akron and the actual location of his Cathedral of Tomorrow. Seated comfortably in lawn chairs at his summer cottage near a local lake, Humbard told me of his early days. His formal education consisted only of high school, but he was the son of a country preacher from the Arkansas hills and was ordained in his father's church. "We were very poor. When we bowed our heads for Sunday dinner, sometimes we had to wait until Wednesday to get it."

He decided to be an evangelist at the age of thirteen after watching a Ringling Brothers Circus set up for a performance. "I compared our ragged old revival tent with theirs and thought, if God had a tent like that he'd have a crowd like that."

Rex's "tent" now sits on a thirty-one acre site. It's a circular domed building one hundred yards in diameter. Suspended from the ceiling is an illuminated cross one hundred feet by fifty feet with nearly five thousand bulbs that have eighty colour changes to match the mood of the service.

When I remarked on the grandeur of the Cathedral of Tomorrow Rex shrugged it off. "It might as well be filled with hay. My job is to get people right with the Lord, not to build round Cathedrals or buy television equipment."

The building of the Cathedral began in 1957 and was plagued with money problems from the beginning. Work went slowly as construction loans proved inadequate in the face of rising costs from last minute changes. He finally received help from an unexpected source. Jimmy Hoffa and the Teamsters Union gave him a 1.2 million dollar mortgage loan and the building was completed. "My interest was solely in getting the loan, not the place from where it came," explained Humbard.

"We have better than two thousand visitors to the Cathedral each week from forty states and Canada. After church they can go next door to the Cathedral Buffet. All you can eat for three dollars. It's open to the public too all through the week. Our Cathedral has mid-week meetings for the church and for the community. I believe in not letting places sit idle. Next door we're building a seven hundred and fifty foot tower copied after your tower in Calgary. We're putting our TV antennae on it but I'm also including a revolving restaurant to get more use out of it.

"You've got to give people what they want. I watch all the reports on our computers here to see what the people like. I want what they want. If next Sunday I could sing anthems instead of country music, and wear striped britches and long tails and high collars and get more people by doing that, then that's what I would do.

"You see those network executives in New York or Toronto or Ottawa don't rub shoulders with the man on the street. They really don't know what he wants. I know that there is a great need for my type of programme, so that's what I give them."

I asked him what he thought of the show business type of religious broadcast, the star studded extravaganzas.

"I don't like to criticize other religious programmes, but all these big spectaculars, with their choreography and scenery and celebrities, is not for me. When you get into something like this you get into working with people who are not involved with the ministry. I feel if a person is involved in religious programming he should be religious."

"What about social issues?" I asked. "With the number of stations you are on it would be an excellent opportunity to speak out on poverty or race relations or the war in Vietnam."

"First of all my people don't want to hear that. My audience is not interested in my views on Vietnam because I am not a military man. I'm a preacher. Do you really feel that I can cure social ills just by talking about them? If I went to put up a sign saying 'Rex Humbard, Surgeon,' but I've never been to medical school, I'd be in trouble. They'd put me in jail. I have no right to intrude upon something I have not been educated in. One of the big problems today is there are too many people just talking about social issues and not doing anything about them, and that's hypocrisy. When we talk so much and do so little, people stop listening. What we have to do is get man right in his heart. That will solve a lot of our social problems."

When I think back to my discussion with Humbard at that time I feel he must have known what was lying ahead in terms of financial difficulties because when I asked him what was the biggest problem he might have with his ministry he answered, "I think mainly trying to do more than I have money or staff to do. I've read the Bible quite a bit and there's no place that says burn the mortgage and rejoice. It says go into all the world and preach the gospel. A lot of people think we're wealthy but the real truth is I have large mortgages and if next week I could make arrangements to re-mortgage to raise more money I would do it in order to buy more television time to reach more people. I guess I overextend myself in that area sometimes."

I found Humbard a very warm and sincere man. He is not hard to like and there is no question of his personal honesty. His wife Maude Aimee, named after an earlier evangelist Aimee Semple Macpherson, is direct. She speaks her mind much to the concern of the public relations staff. We were eating dinner with Rex, Maude Aimee and several of the staff in the Cathedral restaurant when the conversation got around to Canada.

The Humbard's crusade had taken them to every province and Rex was high in his praise for the people, the scenery and the Canadian way of life. Maude Aimee agreed that Canada was a wonderful country, but added "I don't like the idea of your giving shelter to all those draft dodgers. You shouldn't allow them into your country."

"What should be done with them?" I asked.

"If I had my way," she replied, "I'd line them up against the wall and shoot them."

This comment from his wife, especially in front of a television reporter, caused Rex to almost choke on his food as the staff turned several shades of red.

Although Maude Aimee has for years sung on the programme she considers herself first and foremost a wife and mother.

She told me, "There have been some rough times over the years. I first met Rex when I was fifteen and he was a singer and guitar player and we didn't always have enough in terms of material goods. But I always said I'd sooner live in a tent with Rex than to live in a mansion with someone I didn't love. We've had each other and we believe in what we are doing. We have four lovely children and fine grandchildren and that's really all that counts."

It was five years before I met Rex and Maude Aimee again. This time it was in Portsmouth, Virginia where I was filming a *Man Alive* programme with Pat Robertson and his *700 Club*. The Humbards were guests on Robertson's programme one day and we had a chance to renew acquaintances before and after the broadcast.

Rex looked somewhat out of place in this slick atmosphere, a bit like Charlie Farquarson in Las Vegas, but he gamely answered Robertson's rather patronizing questions and applauded obediently when the up tempo singers and musicians performed.

Robertson mixes charm, interviews and testimonials with prayer, phone-in counselling, music and a great deal of forced laughter. The pace is fast, the entertainment level high and the requests for money strident and persistent.

He has formed the Christian Broadcasting Network, which is rapidly challenging the three major American networks in size. He owns some television and radio stations outright and is the only non-profit organization to own a satellite earth station which sends the *700 Club* into seventeen countries around the world.

Robertson told me that he had started his Christian Broadcasting network in 1960 with a three dollar donation and has never looked back.

"Now we have this one hundred and forty-two acre site and are building a twenty-five million dollar broadcasting complex. We will have the most sophisticated TV studios in North America."

I asked about the success of electronic evangelism in general. "I do feel there is a tremendous thrust of revival in North America. Conversions in the United States and Canada are unprecedented in terms of numbers. We are experiencing a great spiritual awakening. The consequence hasn't touched the life of our country as much as we'd like but nonetheless the proliferation of Christian television programmes is evidence of this revival. Now we are pushing overseas. I feel that God is going to use the United States and Canada to mount one of the greatest overseas thrusts of all time."

The transporting of America's religious values to third world countries by satellite is the cause of criticism by some observers of the evangelical scene. Reverend Keith Woollard, Director of Television for the United Church of Canada, comments, "Because these programmes originate in the United States, it means that in other countries, Latin America and the Philippines for example, a lot of folks will identify the Christian way with the American way and I think that's a serious mistake. The danger with these programmes is that they bless the American status quo, 'What's good for General Motors is good for God,' and I don't believe that's true."

Pat Robertson's attitude is similar to Bill Bright's. It's a matter of urgency because the moral decay of the world is increasing every day. Millions of dollars are needed to buy more television time to tell more people about Christ.

I find this kind of broadcast ministry distasteful and at times fraudulent.

The claim that the television evangelist is introducing millions to Christianity is not borne out by the statistics. He is, for the most part, reaching those who are already believers and are open to a more fundamental approach to their faith. He has no tolerance for an understanding of religion that encompasses more than slogans, pat phrases or biblical quotes lifted out of context. I'm sure I would find very little value in a religion that can be summed up on a bumper sticker.

The television evangelist, though proclaiming to be a simple, humble servant of God, is in fact part of the world of big business, completely unrelated to the man he professes to serve. He lives in a world of company jets, liberal expense accounts, multi-million dollar corporate enterprises, with show business celebrity status. "God never meant to go second class," is the answer I often get when I question the life style of the electronic religion baron.

The whole process works because television does such an effective selling job and many people really believe they can buy a better life. When Christ is packaged as slickly as a new deodorant and sold with the promise that "one shot and you're good for eternity" millions reach for their cheque books.

After fifteen years in religious broadcasting and being involved with people of all faiths all over the world I have learned to respect a person's theological position. This respect certainly extends to evangelicals of all faiths, who I applaud for their sincerity and their zeal. But, I do not believe that the medium of broadcasting was meant to be used for commercial gain by any religious sect or its leader, nor do I feel the love of God should be put up for sale. I care about both broadcasting and religion too much for that.